Break THE
LIMITS

PAUL CHRIS SALAAM

This Book is a
Gift

To
_____

From
_____

on occasion
_____

date
_____

BREAK THE LIMITS

Copyright © 2024 Paul Chris Salaam

All rights reserved. No portion of this publication may be reproduced or transmitted in any form or by any means, electronic or mechanical, including photocopy, recording or any information storage and retrieval system without permission in writing from the author and publisher.

LIMITS

CONTENTS

Dedication.   Special thanks   Acknowledgment   Introduction

Character   02   Hate or Love   49

Racism   59

How To Live Fulfilled Life   68   Personal Growth   73

Discipline   8 6

Loyalty   110

Morality   124

God's view on Gender and Sexuality   136

dedication

I specially dedicate this book to the King eternal, immortal, invisible, the only wise God, The One who deserves the honor and glory forever and ever. His grace, mercy, and faithfulness toward me. Without you, I don't know where I would have been today. I am forever grateful. To you be all the glory. Thank you, father, thank you Jesus, and thank you, Holy Spirit.

SPECIAL thanks

It's our sense of value that releases the flow of virtue. I celebrate God's grace on my spiritual father, the Restoration Apostle. Apostle Prof. Johnson Suleman.

Thank you, Daddy, for your tireless work in God's Vineyard. I am grateful for your leadership and confidence in me. My prayer continually for you, Sir, is for Long life, good health, and more Unction to carry on the restoration mandate. Thanks again a billion times, Sir. I treasure & value you always—more grace, Sir.

acknowledgement

To the entire OFM America pastorate. All the members of OFM America, you are a unique bunch. You are all the finest people anywhere on this planet. To my Tulsa branch, the best congregation on this side of eternity. Blessing to you all.

Also, I want to acknowledge my senior pastors in the ministry, Dr. Kingsley Aigbe, Dr. Fidelis Ayemoba, and Dr. Azemhe Azena, etc. I also wish to acknowledge all my friends that made this project possible. Especially Bro Mark time will not permit me to express my sincere appreciation; thank you. To all the "Break the Limit" subscribers and friends. I am grateful to you all. Lastly, and extremely important to my beautiful wifey, God bless you babe.

INTRODUCTION

Breaking Limits - Unlocking Your Full Potential

In life, we often encounter limits – those barriers, obstacles, or even our doubts and fears that hinder us from reaching our God-given potential. These limits are not always obvious or external; they can manifest within us, hidden deep within our thoughts and actions. While some may associate limits with familiar struggles like the temptations of the flesh, such as fornication or adultery, they extend far beyond the surface of our understanding.

In Galatians 5:9, the Bible declares, "A little yeast works through the whole batch of dough." This profound truth highlights how even the smallest hindrance can permeate our entire lives, affecting our growth and potential. But, is it possible to break free from these limitations? Can we transcend the boundaries that confine us?

To break, in its essence, means to separate oneself from those very things that hinder or obstruct our progress. To "break the limit" is to embark on a journey that goes beyond mere expectation – it's a transformative act that bridges the gap between where we are and where we dream of being. It's about courageously crossing the threshold of our comfort zones, setting entirely new standards, and becoming the change we've always sought. It's the audacity to chart a new course in the story of our lives.

This book, the first in a series, has been crafted with one paramount goal in mind: to empower you to actualize your destiny. While the Holy Spirit is unquestionably the preeminent teacher and divine guide He often works through the experiences of people and the materials at our disposal. Just as the Apostle Paul counseled his spiritual son in 2 Timothy 2:2, encouraging him to pass on wisdom to others, we believe you belong to the category of faithful individuals destined to teach and inspire others in their journeys.

Within the pages of this book, you will discover invaluable Insights drawn from both sacred scriptures and the wisdom of great men. Yet, my intention extends beyond mere knowledge acquisition. By His grace, I fervently desire that you become an active practitioner of the principles outlined in this book. Learning, after all, is most profound when it is accompanied by action. So, as you embark on this transformative journey, remember that you are not merely a reader but a participant. More grace, Congratulations, and with open arms, I welcome you to the era of breaking limits. In Life's journey, always remember, that JESUS IS LORD.

Character

Character is your identity. **It's who you are. It's visible to others**

01

Break THE

LIMITS ▶

Character

"Perseverance, character; and character, hope."
Romans 5:4 NIV

"And endurance, proven Character (spiritual maturity); and proven Character, hope, and confident assurance [of eternal salvation" Romans 5:4 (AMP)

What is Character?
Character is a distinctive identity, mental and moral qualities formed over time that defines one's personality. Character is a combination of what we say and how we behave. Isaiah 61:3, Scripture calls us "tree of righteousness."

If we are trees, figuratively speaking, then our Character is the fruit of the tree, and "a tree is known by its fruits." YOU ARE NOT ONLY WHAT YOU SAY; YOU ARE WHAT YOU DISPLAY FOR OTHERS TO SEE. Character is your label. It is attached to your personality like white on rice. Character is the distinctive quality of your moral marker.

A person's Character can be good or bad. Moral or Character is an assessment of an individual's stable moral quality.
Character is your identity. It is who you are. It is visible to others. However, I would like to mention that there are factors which shape or influence our Character.
Let us take a look at some world views here:

   1. Universal truth,

   2. Nature, and

   3. Nurture.

First, what is the Universal truth?
In the context of this book, I define it as a statement, belief, or belief system that corresponds to reality regardless of times and Geographical region. An instance might be twenty is more significant than ten – not exactly profound, but always true. Let us get biblical perspective too. "You reap what you sow" based on Galatians 6:7-9. Another is what is known as the golden rule "Do to others as you will have them,

do to you" Matthew 7:12. When you read Matthew 7:12 King James Version, the last part of the verse reads, "for this is the Law and the Prophets."

That is essentially saying that all the prophets' writings and all biblical laws were established, among other things, and apart from the first commandment, so that we may treat our fellow man/women with dignity.
Another is Acts 20:35 "we must support the weak... 'It is more blessed to give than to receive.
These are beliefs/principles that every civilized people agrees that they are fundamental. The thing about universal truths is, you don't have to have faith in them, but they apply to you nonetheless.

The following example is based on two scriptures Genesis 1:27 God created man in His image". "All men are created equal" based on Acts 17:25-26. American founders, among other things, declared independence on the premise of these universal truths. An excerpt from the Declaration of Independence July 4, 1776 "We hold these truths to be self-evident, that all men are created equal, that they are endowed by their Creator with certain unalienable Rights, that among these are Life, Liberty and the pursuit of Happiness." Although these truths were made popular by the American founding fathers, they are not an American idea; they are universal truths based on God's word. Laws and cultures have been molded and shaped according to these universal truths. They will continue to do so in the foreseeable future. These laws and cultures created by these truths affect all of us. The last examples are "forgive, and you will be forgiven" Matthew 6:14. Caring Mathew 25:40. Self-respect Ephesians 5:29, Job 12:3, truthfulness 2 Cor 8:21, 2 Timothy 2:15, Colossians 3:9, and Loyalty Proverbs 17:17, Mathew 26:35. "Everyone must respect the rule of law" Romans 13:1-5, Titus 3:1, Romans 2:13, 1

Peter 2:13-17, Luke 20:25. These and others measured above are universal truths that have the exact exchange rate everywhere. They are the bedrock of western civilization and civilization itself. Everyone is expected to live and behave according to these truths regardless of region, political affiliation, or socioeconomic status.

I believe this to be true; sometimes, adversity can help to mold someone's Character. It can bring the best or worst out of anyone. It all depends on how we handle it. Hebrew 5:8 "...Jesus learned obedience through the things he suffered." I have seen situations where a person went through pain and hurt, came out of it without being bitter, and I see cases also where others went through the same situation, but the results are different. One came out bitter, the other came out better. One chooses to forgive. The other decides to hold on to their hurts. It is not comfortable, but it is true character can be formed in adversity and that is a universal truth. Choose to master your situation instead of it mastering you. You have the choice to be pragmatic or sarcastic, and that's the truth.

Second thing; NATURE:
Some things just come naturally to us. For instance, when someone smiles at you, it is natural to smile back at them. Also, it is natural when someone is in trouble to cry out to God. Even though some don't believe in God, there is something deep within all humans that compels us to call on nature's God. It is instinctive. We are born with certain qualities; for example, everyone is born with love in their hearts. God put that in all of us, but family, friends, and society taught us discrimination and other negative character traits over time. How do I know this? Simple!

Scriptures say that "God is Love" 1 John 4:16, and we were created in His image and moral likeness Gen 1:26- 27 if God is love, which He is because the Bible says so, that means we are made and designed as a reservoir of love. He intends for us to be a conduit (channel) of love by positively touching others. That is nature's God's plan for our lives to display is infinite love for humankind.

Thirdly, NURTURE:
in this context, means things we were taught or things we encourage to grow that are now part of who we are. Most of our character trait is as a result of Nurture or Manmade. All of the negative things we learned as youngsters and some we still practice today were taught to us. A child is taught to be a bigot; he was not born that way but was brainwashed to think everyone is inferior. A child is also programmed and

conditioned to believe he is better than everyone. Others are trained to hate certain classes or races of people. Some are nurtured to think that certain classes of people are sub-humans.

Others fabricate lies to solidify a position on race, gender, economic background, political affiliation, socioeconomic status, etc. Those were self-taught, or others taught us to uphold those views or opinions. Nurture is deliberate on the part of others and haphazard (lacking any obvious principle of organization) on the part of most. The Holocaust is an example of Nurture. Racial discrimination is an example of Nurture. Religious discrimination is an example of Nurture, and Tribal discrimination is an example of Nurture.

Attitude toward people because of their physical disability, cultural orientation, or place of origin are examples of nurture. The idea or belief that some people should not have access to specific neighborhoods, material resources, networks, wealth, and connections even when qualified is Nurture. The attribute that makes us judge people and conclude on them before getting to know them. Also, nurture is writing off people for flimsy reasons and having shallow opinions about them.
Compromising our values to blend with others when we know it's wrong. How could something so ephemeral (short-term) or trivial (of little value) undergird our sense of self-worth?

Nurture is also known as Mentorship. A Christian i.e. one who believes in Jesus Christ and accepts His LORDSHIP and Yields to His instructions and direction, knows Nurture as Discipleship. The absence of right Nurture (God's word) is when destructive norms are left unchallenged overtime. Nurture is the act of gaining information that begins from Cradle and ends to the grave. Nurture can be overt or covert. Great leaders are raised by Nurture. The music we listen to, the movies or series we watch, and the books we read. The people we idolize all nurture us. Nurture is the basis for education, entertainment, politics, and economics. Nurture determines the world's direction. If you want a specific outcome, you must nurture and breed for that. Nurture is direction, control, molding, character hacking, etc.

When destructive norms are left unchallenged over time, they develop into bad habits, and bad habits become bad Characters. We must, and we need to challenge certain things like racism, sexism, and religious bigotry. Flawed Characters such as selfishness, hate, self- centeredness, and lack of empathy must be challenged.

All these are character traits that affect others. It's said that it is hard to teach an old dog new tricks, but it is not impossible. I believe that an old dog can learn new things if it tries. Just give it time.

First, let us hear the bad news! The bad news is: you cannot change your Character by what you wear. A man or woman with a flawed character could wear a $2500 suit and wear the best makeup and fanciest wristwatch, yet it does not change who they are underneath the glamour. Their Character remains the same even under disguise. When given the opportunity, it will show up. Now the good news is you can alter your Character by a seven-letter word CHOICES: You can choose love, over hate, peace, over conflict, or you can choose faith over fear. You can replace irresponsibility with responsibility, respect over disrespect, principle over lack of code. You can choose empathy, over indifference and being aloof, fairness over bias, caring over cruelty, and spirituality over carnality. You can choose to respect or rebel against authority, or you can choose a healthy dose of the fear of God. IT'S A CHOICE! Trust me! I understand! It's not easy to unlearn wrong things or typical behaviors, but we can unlearn unhealthy characters and develop healthy ones. It all starts with the choices that we make.

In Acts 6:4 & 7, but we will give ourselves continually

to prayer and the ministry of the word." Then the word of God spread, and the number of the disciples multiplied greatly in Jerusalem. A great many of the priests were obedient to the faith.

It was the choice the apostles made to give themselves to prayers and ministry of the word. The outcome was that the message kept on spreading, and the disciples' number continued to increase. It all started with the choice they made. Today, many in Christendom are waiting for God to do everything for them, including making a change that God has placed in their hands. Brother, Sister God cannot do for us what He expects us to do for ourselves. I know some will say, what about the role of the Holy Spirit? Many fail to realize that the Holy Spirit is our Helper; according to John 14:26, He can only help us when we align with him. For example, the Holy Spirit can help you pass a test if you study for it.

Joshua 15: 24 NLT "But if you refuse to serve the Lord, then CHOOSE today whom you will serve. Would you prefer the gods your ancestors served beyond the Euphrates? Or will it be the gods of the Amorites in whose land you now live? But as for my family and me, we will serve the Lord."

The keyword in this verse is "CHOOSE" in making a character choice; choose to change for yourself and your loved one. You are the most significant factor, and I believe you can do it. God is waiting on you; your family is waiting on you. The world is waiting on you. The man/woman who resides inside of you is waiting to introduce himself to you. However, choice is the first step for meeting that new individual you were meant to be. We need to get to a place in our walk with God. Were we experience what the lexicon dictionary calls "evidential" proofs. An evidential display of the Characters of Christ at work in our life. In short, we need to get to a place where we do not have to tell people we are Christians; they can see that we are. Good Character can be developed. Here are some character builders.

"But the fruit of the Spirit is love, joy, peace, forbearance, kindness, goodness, faithfulness, gentleness, and self-control. Against such things, there is no law." Galatians 5:22-23 (NIV)

Love, Joy, Peace, Patience or forbearance, kindness, Goodness, Faithfulness, Gentleness, and self-control are attributes of the Holy Spirit and excellent character builders. They can be developed through the help of the Holy Ghost and self-discipline. We must be deliberate in our pursuit of the God kind of character. As much as they are the attributes of the Holy Spirit that should be on display in the life of Christian who has being touched by God. I have seen in the lives of many Christians today that profess to have had an encounter with God but, these characters are lacking. One of the reasons is that many mistakes gifting as a sign of good character. The fact is clear your gift or gifts can take you to the top but only character can keep you on top. In this chapter, we are going to be discussing these builders.

LOVE: I define Love as doing and binding (Putting together) the best for others' best interest. Love is the most significant character builder; without it, everything falls apart. It is the foundation of a great character. Everyone has the capacity, and ability to love. Even a hardened criminal can love. It is in our DNA makeup. However, it takes the help of the Holy Spirit to empower us to walk in God-kind of Love. This type of Love referred to as the "Agape love," the relentless Love, the kind of Love with faith in people and hope always. That is Love; it never give up on people. It is the type of Love that pulls people from the depth of hell. The kind of Love with unlimited capacity to forgive. Paul writing to the troubled church in the city of Corinth he wrote:

1 Corinthians 13:1- 3 "If I speak in the tongues of men or angels, but do not have Love, I am only a

resounding gong or a clanging cymbal. 2 If I have the gift of prophecy and can fathom all mysteries and all knowledge, and if I have a faith that can move mountains, but does not have Love, I am nothing. 3 If I give all I possess to the poor and give over my body to hardship that I may boast, but do not have Love, I gain nothing."

The next verses of scriptures give us the description of what's God kind of love is. 1 Corinthians 13: 4-7

4 Love is patient; Love is kind. It does not envy; it does not boast; it is not proud. 5 It does not dishonor others, it is not self-seeking, it is not easily angered, it keeps no record of wrongs. 6 Love does not delight in evil but rejoices with the truth. 7 It always protects, always trusts, always hopes, always perseveres.

Verse eighth speaks of the supremacy of Love over everything.

8 Love never fails. But where there are prophecies, they will cease; where there are tongues, they will be stilled; where there is knowledge, it will pass away.

Wow! "Love never fails," meaning that Love is our reset bottom. When all fails, Love, even when it's not convenient, because Love never fails.

Verse 11 When I was a child, I talked like a child, I thought like a child, I reasoned like a child.

When I became a man, I put the ways of childhood behind me. The walk of a believer is a love walk Ephesians 5:2.

Speaking on 1 Corinthians 13:11, let's put it like this: when I was a child in my Love walk, I speak and act like a child. I understood as a child now that I matured in Love. I must exhaust Love instead of condemning people. It is a worthy saying; you cannot hate until you have exhausted Love. The fact is you cannot exhaust the God-kind of Love. Agape love is unconditional love. Unconditional Love is a sign of maturity. The believer's walk is a walk of love. Love is the lifeblood of the universe. Love powers every living thing. It was and still is the reason Christ died for the sins of the world. John 3:16 "for God so love the world that he gave..." it's said that "you can give without loving but, you cannot Love without giving" The nature of God is Love 1 John 4:8 Love entails sacrifice. Romans 5:8 God demonstrates his love for us in this: While we were still sinners, Christ died for us. Love is the essence of the human spirit. Whoever does not love does not know God; you can't experience the real kind of Love without knowing the creator, and you can't encounter the creator and lack His kind of Love. Scriptures teach 1 Corn 13:13, and now these three remain faith, hope, and Love. But the greatest of these is Love. Faith is a powerful force, but its power is limited and diminished without Love. Now, remain after all is said and made three things faith, hope, and Love. What trumped the two is Love. An excellent character builder.

Pray this with me. Dear God, help me to love others as you love them.

JOY: Isaiah 12:3 Therefore with joy you will draw water from the wells of salvation

You cannot be an effective person without Joy and you cannot buy Joy on Amazon or eBay. No!! Real or Genuine Joy cannot be purchased with money. It is priceless. As the above scriptures stated, "With Joy will you draw water out of the wells of salvation" Wells of salvation in this scripture speaks of the levels of His presence, and water speaks of both the Holy Spirit and the word of God. In scriptures, THE WORD OF GOD refers to water. Many references here are examples.
Ephesians 5:26" Paul making a comparison of the relationship of the husband and wife to that's of Christ, and the Church states; "that He might" speaking of Jesus "sanctify and cleanse her" speaking of the church "with the washing of water by the WORD. Putting those two together, Isaiah 12:3 means that you cannot get revelation from the Holy Spirit if you lack Joy. The character of Joy is a missing link in many lives today.

May God give you pure joy in Jesus' name! Joy is not as a result of happenings. No my friend, that's happiness. Happiness is a result of happenings. Joy has nothing to do with happenings. Someone can be down and out according to human standards and still have Joy.

Dorothy Norwood's song comes into mind "I still have joy, I still have Joy, after, all I have been through I still have joy." Joy is expressive and visible. The characters of the Holy Spirit are descriptive. The essence of Joy is unexplainable; why is it unexplainable? Because Joy comes from knowing and obeying Jesus. Joy was such a vital tool in David's life and ministry he had to beg God to restore it when he lost it through disobedience. Psalm 51:12 Restore to me the joy of your salvation and uphold me by your generous Spirit. It is interesting to know that Joy comes after Love and before peace. The reason I believe you cannot have real joy without Love, and you can't effectively work in harmony without Joy. Joy is the only cure for sadness and depression. Jesus is the true giver of Joy through the person of the Holy Spirit. Joy is contagious when you have it; it shows, even in challenging times its shines through.

Pray this with me: Jesus, please, increase my Joy in Jesus' name.

PEACE: the ability to be calm in the midst of a storm. Peace is an important asset and can be a vital tool for a healthy relationship. Scriptures teach us that we must seek peace and pursue it. Psalms 43:14 Depart from evil, and do good; seek peace, and pursue it. To pursue means to follow to catch even if it eludes you. You are to chase after it. As a believer, you must be a channel that helps bring peace to the world around

you, but you can't give what you don't have. That's where the Holy Spirit comes in. Jesus is the real giver of peace via the Holy Ghost's connection, and when your peace is disturbed, it hurts Him. One of the names of Jesus is the "prince of peace" Isaiah 9:6...His name shall be called the Prince of peace. Mathew 5:9 blessed are the peacemakers: for they shall be called the children of God. Children of God are peacemakers. That is what they are known for, peacemaking; you cannot profess Christianity and be hostile or antagonistic to your
fellow man that does not fit the picture of a true believer.
Pursue peace, and you will live in peace and be known for making and keeping the peace.

Prayer: Pray this with me, my dear prince of peace; help me live and walk in peace with myself and others.

PATIENCE or forbearance: I define patience as the ability and capacity to tolerate others even when they deserve abandonment. A patient person does not rush into things or conclude on a matter till he/she has first thoroughly researched it. He is not quick to judgment with a statement from one person; He listens carefully to both sides and decides on accurate information. It would be best if you did not give up on your son or daughter easily neither cave-in out of pressure. A patient person stays on point despite the pressure to give in or give up. He/she is not moving by trends or toss by the winds of popularity. A patient woman does not give up on her husband because he has fallen on hard times and struggles to make ends meet. A patient friend will not change his friend because he is rich and famous, and his friend is still struggling to pay his/her rent. He has forgotten that was the friend who was there for him in times of need. A patient man does not end years of marriage because of frivolous accusations; a patient man/woman stays with you for the long haul. They do not give up easily. Who is your Example of patience? Scriptures give us the perfect role model. In Hebrews 12:2, the Bible tells us to look to "Jesus the author and finisher of our faith who for the joy that was set before him endured the cross, despising the shame, and is set down at the right hand of the throne of God. It's incredible what the character of patience can do "He endured the cross" despised and embarrassed by sinners. Because of His patience, He is now seated at the right hand of God's power. Hallelujah!!!! Praise the Lord.

Prayer: Lord, give me patience in Jesus's name.

KINDNESS: Online dictionary defines kindness as the quality of being friendly, generous, and considerate. A kind person is forgiving. Never keep records of wrong.

Strive to obey the golden rule. "in everything, do to others what you would have them do to you, for this sums up the Law and the Prophets" Matthew 7:12. A kind man/woman is not abrasive; she is aware and respect others feelings and let them express their opinion. A kind person accepts others' differences, welcomes them, and he or she is not imposing. A kind person does not crucify others because of how they look, sound, and talk. A kind person does not discriminate because of political affiliation, place of origin, or the tribe to which he/she belongs. She is considerate and speaks well of others despite differences. A kind person doesn't seek to be disagreeable.

Prayer: My father, my father in Jesus' name, help me to be kind to all people.

GOODNESS: Online dictionary defines goodness as the quality of being morally good or virtuous. A Good person never undermines others' progress. He wishes and prays for others' success. A good man/woman rejoices when others rejoice and cry when they cry. A good person is generous at heart and generous materially (He/she is a giver). A good man helps people and never asks for reward or recognition. He believes doing well to others is its reward. He/she gets trills in assisting people prosper Acts 10:38.

Prayer: Lord, my helper, help me do well without asking for a reward.

FAITHFULNESS: Is the ability to be devoted or loyal despite countless opportunities to be unfaithful or disloyal. A faithful person BELIEVES IN OTHERS; he is consistent and truthful. His Word is his bond. A faithful person is transparent. A faithful person is an authentic person. A faithful individual is a real person; a faithful person can be trusted. You can count on them in times of need. You know their moral standard; they do not allow money to compromise them. Faithfulness can also be defined as integrity. Integrity came from the Word integers. Integers are numbers that can be written without fractions. Integers are whole numbers 99.999...% is not 100. 2+2=4 that it is a fact does not matter how much we want 2+2 to be 6. A half-truth is a complete lie. Faithfulness or integrity is a character that you have, or you don't. The Holy Spirit is our helper, teacher, Comforter, and counselor, etc. The Holy Spirit is all of that but, He expects us to be deliberately faithful. Thank God, anyone can be faithful through conscious effort and deliberate actions. The Holy Spirit can help you, yes but, He needs you to be intentional. By avoiding things or people that will cause you to compromise your morals. Stop going to places that feed on your weakness.

Prayer: In Jesus's name Lord, help me to be faithful in ALL THINGS

GENTLENESS: This is the quality of being kind,

tender-hearted, and calm. A gentle individual is not into power tussle or muscle-flexing. He is sure of himself; most people have underrated and misunderstood this character builder. Many mistake gentleness for weakness; that's a real fallacy because gentle people have immense strength. They choose not to flex it unnecessarily. Real power is to have the strength and restrain oneself from abusing it. That's leads us to the next character builder, self-control.

SELF-CONTROL is the ability to show restraint when others do not expect you to. To exercised Control over one's own emotions, impulses, or desires. The ability to regulate one's responses to avoid an undesirable outcome. The power to increase desirable behavior and achieve long time success. Self-control is a character that was prominent in the ministry of the Lord Christ.

Hebrews 4:15 For we have not a high priest which cannot be touched with the feeling of our infirmities; but was in all points tempted like as we are, yet without sin.

The amplified rendered it like this "For we do not have a High Priest who is unable to sympathize and understand our weaknesses and temptations, but One who has been tempted [knowing exactly how it feels to

be human] in every respect as we are, yet without [committing any] sin." Hebrew 4:15

"He was tempted yet without sin" the Lord was brought before Pilate in Isaiah 53:7. Scriptures tell us that "...He was oppressed and afflicted, yet he did not open his mouth..." self-control is the ability to know when to act like a lion or a lamb. Most people think that you are supposed to answer your opponent always. That is exhausting your mental energy and a waste of your precious time.

Sometimes your silence is enough to send them a message. Self-control is a dangerous weapon against the opposition and a useful asset. It's a vital character builder. When we talk about self-control, one thing comes to mind "Lust."

WHAT IS LUST?

Lust is a strong spiritual force that produces a profound or intense dark desire for someone or something. One can Lust after anything, e.g., someone can lust for food, expensive clothing, pieces of jewelry or cars, etc. Lust is the catalyst of greed. It unloosens the human spirit. God's word forbids both Lust and greed. God's word cautions us in1 John 2:15-17, "do not love the world or anything in the world. If anyone loves the world, love for the Father is not in them. 16 For everything in the world-the lust of the flesh, the lust of the eyes, and the pride of life—comes not from the Father but from the world. 17 The world and its desires pass away, but whoever does the will of God lives forever."

The ability to control oneself is an attribute of the Holy Spirit and a marker (character) of a spirit-filled believer. Lust is never beneficial to the soul and always leads to destructive outcomes. It's the basis for man's excommunication (Exiled) from the Garden of God (Eden). Adam was given a strict command not to eat of "the fruit of the tree in the midst of the garden" they disobeyed and ate. Through their disobedience, a byproduct of Lust, they brought about the fall of humankind. The scriptures read thus;

For God knows that on the day you eat from it, your eyes will be opened [that is, you will have greater awareness], and you will be like God, knowing [the difference between] good and evil."

And when the woman saw that the tree was good for food and that it was delightful to look at, and a tree to be desired in order to make one wise and insightful, she took some of its fruit and ate it; and she also gave some to her husband with her, and he ate. Genesis 3:5-6

The next verse was the outcomes of them acting on their Lust. Therefore, the Lord God sent Adam away from the Garden of Eden to till and cultivate the ground from which he was taken. Genesis 3:6

Notice Adam and Eve were all these things the Devil told them they could become if they give heed to their impulse. They were already gods, wiser than angels, which Lucifer was part of Psalm 82:1/6& John 10:34-35. They knew what was right from wrong because God almighty was their teacher Gen 2:17. They were wise and insightful because Adam gave name to all the animals that God created in Gen 2:20. That is what can happen with sexual Lust; the Devil tells men/women that whatever the object of their desire has, their spouse does not have it. The Devil taunts people with lies; he says things like, why don't you test it this one time only? I am sure it will not hurt you before you know it you are hooked; and you are in all kinds of trouble because you listened to his lies.

Prayer: I speak to your right now; you are free from the spirit of Lust by the blood of Jesus, in Jesus name Amen.

There are three killers of great men/women. I call

them the trinity of destruction;

1. The Lust for money, 2. The Lust for power, and the last one measured above 3. Lust for the opposite sex.

Many today have taken their Lust for money to an absurd Height and will do and say anything to acquire money to the extent of selling their soul for dollars. Their Lust for money has no bounds Scriptures declares;

1 Timothy 6:10 King James Version (KJV)

For the love of money is the root of all evil: which while some coveted after, they have erred from the faith, and pierced themselves through with many sorrows.

Please take note, the scriptures did not say money is the root of all evil. It says the love of money is the root of all kinds of evil. The reason is that money itself has no form or personality. It derives the character or persona of the one that possesses it. Therefore, if someone that Lust after money acquires money, he will use it to fulfill his/her lustful purposes. When a bad man has money, he uses it to do bad things, and when a good man has money, he uses it to do good things. It takes their personalities. No one with a lust for money ever ends well. In the end, they always crash; it doesn't matter how high their Lust for money takes them; it always brings them back down because money is a good slave but a cruel master. Some lust after money and has wandered from God and eventually destroyed themselves; craving for money affects both the church and the world. For Example, a very famous American businessman stole $65billion in the biggest Ponzi scheme in history. He was sentenced to 150 years in prison. Today in God's house, some ministers are into the Ponzi scheme. They are swapping dollars for prayers. The church has copied from the world instead of the world copying from the church. Lord help us!

Prayer: My father in Jesus' name, money will not control me; I will control money.

Next is "POWER" many are so power conscious they are willing to compromise their value to secure it. Many believers today, because of their Lust for power, have departed from the faith and give heed to seducing spirit and doctrines of devils; they had blurred the moral line to an extent they no longer can recognize good from evil. Adolf Hitler of Germany, Joseph Stalin of Russia, and Mao Zedong of China, to name a few, are examples of what Lust for power can do to the human soul. These three men are responsible for the death of millions of people in their lifetime. Now you may say I can never be like them, that may be true, but every life that Lust for power has ruined is one too many.

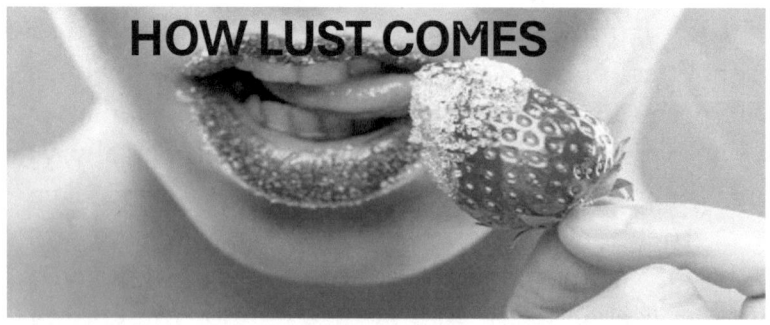

HOW LUST COMES

Let no one say when he is tempted, "I am being tempted by God" [for temptation does not originate from God, but from our own flaws]; for God cannot be tempted by [what is] evil, and He Himself tempts no one. 14 But each one is tempted when he is dragged away, enticed and baited [to commit sin] by his own [worldly] desire (lust,

passion). 15 Then when the illicit desire has conceived, it gives birth to sin; and when sin has run its course, it gives birth to death. James 1:13-15 Amplified.

The desire for sexual gratification drives sexual Lust. Felling tempted is not necessary the same as sinning. Temptations tell us to do things that we should not do. To be tempted is not a sin but to fall into temptations is a sin. Genesis 4:7 "...sin is ready to attack you. That sin will want to control you, but you must control it". I love that "it wants to control you, but you must control it" other versions say master it. Lust generally comes according to scriptures <u>when evil desire drags someone</u>, <u>enticed and baited them to commit sin</u>.

HOW TO OVERCOME SEXUAL LUST & LUST IN GENERAL

1. WAIT ON THE LORD

Lamentations 3:24-28 New International Version (NIV)
24 I say to myself, "The Lord is my portion; therefore I will wait for him."
25 The Lord is good to those whose hope is in him, to the one who seeks him;
26 it is good to wait quietly for the salvation of the Lord.
27 It is good for a man to bear the yoke while he is young.
28 Let him sit alone in silence, for the Lord has laid it on him.

These verses are for everyone, especially for singles,

"wait for Him" singlehood is a gift from God. As a single, you must not waste your time pursuing instant gratification and missed the opportunity of spending time with the Lord. Whether you are young or young at heart, the season of singlehood is one of the best times to seek God. Verse 24 say, "Wait on Him," that significant God knows what you want and need. The next verse says the Lord is good to those that hope in him. The New KJV put it like this "The Lord is good to those that wait on him. "You cannot wait on God and be disappointed. The Lord has given you grace for today. His grace is available for every day of your life; we receive and maintain that grace by having a consistent prayer life. Luke 18:1 says that we must "always pray" without taking a break. Wait in the place of prayers, and fasting is vital in overcoming lust. When your flesh dies in the Alter of prayers and fasting, your spirit comes alive. There must be no need to compromise your character to get ahead in life; it doesn't worth it. Know this; God is for you, and He is always with you John 20:21.

2. FEED ON GOD'S WORD"

Jeremiah 15:16 (NKJV) "Your words were found, and I eat them."

There used to be a commercial on TV with this punch

line "put good in, get good out." Naturally speaking, your diet determines your health. Likewise, spiritually your spiritual food/diet determines your spiritual health. What you take in determines what you give out. When you eat God's Word, it occupies your mind & heart. When those organs are affected spiritually, it alters the trajectory of your soul. The most effective way to change a man's behavior is to change his thought. Scriptures declare in; Psalm 119:11(TLB), "I have thought much about your words and stored them in my heart so that they would hold me back from sin." God's Word has the potency to hold us back from sin when we store His Word in our heart through studying, meditating on the Word, reading Holy Ghost-inspired material, and listening to spirit-filled messages. When we study God's Word, we exchange our thoughts for his thoughts. If you must change, it starts with you changing your thinking, and you can achieve that by engaging God's Word.

3. HAVE AN ACCOUNTABILITY PARTNER

Being accountable is a significant aspect in overcoming lust. While prayer and fasting are essential, a vital tool many believers today are overlooking is the part of being accountable. Accountability and mentorship play a crucial role in overcoming the flesh. I have the privilege to pastor, and I know for a fact that accountability and mentorship is seriously lacking in the body of Christ; scriptures tell us in James 5:15-16

"And the prayer offered in faith will make the sick person well; the Lord will raise them up. If they have sinned, they will be forgiven. Therefore confess your sins to each other and pray for each other so that you may be healed. The prayer of a righteous person is powerful and effective." We certainly know this scripture was written by James, the brother of the Lord to the Hebrews church that was scattered abroad. He was telling them what accountability can do for them. "Confess your faults/sins to each other and pray for each other so that you may be healed."

The proper accountability partner or partners helps us increase commitment and give the clarity to continue on the right part. Being accountable keeps us honest; it's empowered to follow through with our obligation to do the right thing. When we are held accountable, we are more careful in how we act or behave.

3. STOP TEMPTING YOURSELF. LEARN TO STOP SEEKING OUT THINGS WHICH MAKES YOU LUSTFUL.

Job 31:1 (NIV)
"I made a covenant with my eyes not to look lustfully at a young woman.

Songs of Solomon 8:4 (Amplified)
"I command you to take an oath, O daughters of Jerusalem, that you do not rouse nor awaken my love until she pleases.

Song of Solomon 8:4 (KJV)

I charge you, O daughters of Jerusalem, that ye stir not up nor awake my love until he, please.

The Holy Spirit is our helper, but scripture tells us that He cannot help without our permission. The Holy Spirit will never force Himself on us. Job 31:1 Job, a man without the Holy Ghost in him speaking here, said, "I made a covenant with my eyes." If Job did it, you could do much more. Job realizes that you can't un-see things you have seen. Pornography is a big problem in our world today. According to one statistic, there are 1.3million Porn-site on the internet. The porn industry worldwide is a $97 billion industry that's more than the economy of some countries. In the U.S alone, it's a $13 billion industry. Every second over $3000 is spent on pornographic content. The problem is pervasive even in the church. According to Barna Group survey 2016, "76% of 18- to 24-year-old Christians actively seek out porn". True research 2012 states that "71% of teens hide their online behavior from their parents" Parents need to watch out. Over 60% of men watch porn daily". About 50% of committed men and 40% of women watch porn.

Until you take that step, God would not take action. It all starts with you. If it were impossible, it would not be in the scriptures, and as a matter of truth, nothing is impossible with God Luke 1:37. Make that covenant today, and He will help you to keep it. Enter a covenant with the Holy Spirit today to help you stop seeking things that cause lust.

Prayer: By the power of the blood of Jesus, I make a

covenant today not to seek out things that make me lustful, in Jesus' name, Amen.

The next verse says, "Do not rouse nor awaken my love." King James Translations says, "Ye stir not up nor awake my love" why because? Love is such a strong emotion when you awake it outside of the context of marriage or outside your matrimonial home. It burns everything around you. Why rush to taste the thing that you will soon enjoy as much as you want in the proper context (Marriage)? Why cheat when you have a blessing at home (Wife/husband)?
Arousing love before it is ready is a Pandora Box, and its consequences can be disastrous. E.g., a famous American preacher was caught in a scandalous relationship, which ended his ministry. He lost his credibility and everything he had, including his family. Stop going to places that you know are a temptation to you. Stop seeking things that push you to sin. Stop encourage or patronizing individual that drives you to unrighteousness. My friends, one-minute pleasure does not worth your whole future.

4. PRACTICE HOLINESS AND FEAR OF GOD.

HOW TO PRACTICE HOLINESS

Leviticus 20:7

You shall consecrate yourselves therefore and be holy; for I am the Lord your God.

1 Peter 1:16

because it is written, "You shall be holy (set apart), for I am holy."

"Be Holy" is not a suggestion. It's a command that every living soul must obey. It is not left to preachers or governments to dictates what that means. God's commands are not open for debates or suggestions. If we want to access His presence continually, Holiness is the requirement. Here is how to practice Holiness:

a. *Spend time daily in prayers.*

We practice Holiness by living holy through the help of the Holy Spirit & asking God through prayers to help us thirst for more of His Holiness. The more time we spend in His presence, the less appetite we will have for the things of the flesh. Any time you see yourself lusting or mind-wandering, where it is not supposed to, pray for at least three hours. Why three hours? At three hours, the flesh will begin to calm down. Our flesh hates spiritual exercises because they are beneficial to our spirit-man or spiritual life.

"godliness is profitable unto all things, having promise of the life that now is, and of that which is to come" 1 Timothy 4:8b

b. *Speaking in Tongues.*

Jude 20 "But you, beloved, build yourselves up on [the foundation of] your most holy faith [continually progress, rise like an edifice higher and higher], pray in the Holy Spirit."

When we speak with tongues, we build our spirit-man, and when our spirit-man is built up. It helps us resist temptations.

When we build our spirit, man & we align ourselves with the Holy Ghost by silencing our flesh through the mystery of speaking in tongues. Praying in a known language is good but sometimes not effective enough. The most efficient way of praying is in other tongues, aka praying in the Holy Ghost. It's the sure way to align the human spirit with the Holy Spirit.

c. *Be proactive against sinful thoughts & behaviors.*

Every temptation starts with the mind or thought realm. It's conceived in the mind before its manifest in the physical or physical realm. Do this every time you notice your mind wandering, thinking thoughts contrary to God's word cast it out with the word. The Devil is blind, deaf, dumb, and mad. He needs your eyes to see, your ears to hear, your mouth to speak, and your mind to think. That's why He always tries to use your faculties (your inherent mental or physical powers) to carry out his evil plans. Please don't let him; he has no power until we allow him. The weakness in the human flesh is the Devil's strength. Always remember this, you can put your flesh under the power of the Holy Spirit Gal 5:16 & 24. Anytime he starts messing with your mind. Answer him with the word of God. He fears the word of God. Tell Him, Satan! This evil thought is not mine in the name of Jesus; get out! Bible says in 2 Corinthians 10:5,

Casting down imaginations, and every high thing that exalteth itself against the knowledge of God, and bringing into captivity every thought to the obedience of Christ; (King James Version)

We are destroying sophisticated arguments and every exalted and proud thing that sets itself up against the [true] knowledge of God, and we are taking every thought and purpose captive to the obedience of Christ" (Amplified Version).

Tell him, you serpent! These evil imaginations and arguments originated from you. Therefore, I reject it and send it back to you in Jesus' name, amen. Please recognize this; temptation is a suggestion that is waiting for your approval. Please don't give in to it!

Let that Devil know what the Bible teaches in Philippians 4:8 "Finally, brethren, whatsoever things are true, whatsoever things are honest, whatsoever things are just, whatsoever things are pure, whatsoever things are lovely, whatsoever things are of good report; if there be any virtue, and if there be any praise, think on these things."

Speak to the Flesh and Satan. Let them know these are your thoughts: true things, honest things, pure things, lovely things. Things that are of good report, things that bring honor to God, things that glorify God are the things you think on.

He may persist with more suggestions maintain your ground. The more he pushes, you push back! Here is one of the many weaknesses of the Devil. Most people don't know that Satan GIVES UP! He gets tired! Don't let any preacher tell you otherwise. The Devil hates rejection, and he gets weary. Jehovah God Almighty is the only personality that is incapable of being tired John 5:17. Many think Satan never gives up because they didn't stay in the fight long enough to see him run away. You can wear him out by being a proactive Christian.

The Devil and his minions (demons) do not have the Jurisdiction or legal right to exercise authority on earth; they need human for that. We are the ones with the legal power to exercise authority on Earth. Be proactive!

d   Stay with the word daily.

Joshua 1:8 8 This Book of the Law shall not depart from your mouth, but you shall read [and meditate on] it day and night, so that you may be careful to do [everything] in accordance with all that is written in it; for then you will make your way prosperous, and then you will be [a]successful.

Making a way is your responsibility, and living a Holy life is your responsibility also. You may ask how pastor. Scriptures declare, "This Book of the Law shall not depart from your mouth, but you shall read [and meditate on] it day and night" that's a vital key in practicing Holiness.

d.   2 Corinthians 3:18 And we all, with unveiled face, continually seeing as in a mirror the Glory of the Lord, are progressively being transformed into His image from [one degree of] glory to [even more] Glory, which comes from the Lord, [who is] the spirit.

The more we read, study, meditate, and practice God's word, the more we become like Jesus. The word of God is the mirror into the image of God. As we consistently look into this mirror, we are being transformed into the likeness of Abba's father, from one stage of Glory to the next Glory!!!

e. The mystery of fasting.

Biblical Fasting kills our flesh and actives our spirit-man. Isaiah 58:3-12 shows us what that looks like.

Verse 3. Why have we fasted,' they say, 'and You do not see it? Why have we humbled ourselves and You do not notice?' Hear this [O Israel], on the day of your fast [when you should be grieving for your sins] you find something you desire [to do], And you force your hired servants to work [instead of stopping all work, as the law teaches].

4   The facts are that you fast only for strife and brawling and to strike with the fist of wickedness. You do not fast as you do today to make your voice heard on high.

5   Is a fast such as this what I have chosen, a

day for a man to humble himself [with sorrow in his soul]?

Is it only to bow down his head like a reed and to make sackcloth and ashes as a bed [pretending to have a repentant heart]? Do you call this a fast and a day pleasing to the Lord?

6   [Rather] is this not the fast which I choose, to undo the bonds of wickedness, to tear to pieces the ropes of the yoke, to let the oppressed go free And break apart every [enslaving] yoke?

7   Is it not to divide your bread with the hungry and bring the homeless poor into the house; When you see the naked, that you cover him, and not to hide yourself from [the needs of] your own flesh and blood?

Benefits of God's prescribed Fasting verse eight to twelve:

8   Then your light will break out like the dawn, and your healing (restoration, new life) will quickly spring forth; your righteousness will go before you [leading you to peace and prosperity], The Glory of the Lord will be your rear guard.

9   Then you will call, and the Lord will answer; you will cry for help, and He will say, 'Here I Am.' If

you take away from your midst the yoke [of oppression], the finger pointed in scorn [toward the oppressed or the godly], and [every form of] wicked (sinful, unjust) speech,

10   And if you offer yourself to [assist] the hungry and satisfy the [a]need of the afflicted, Then your light will rise in darkness, and your gloom will become like midday.

11   And the Lord will continually guide you, and satisfy your soul in scorched and dry places, And give strength to your bones; you will be like a watered garden, and like a spring of water whose waters do not fail.

Please, note verse eleven "the Lord will continually guide you and satisfy your soul in scorched and dry places, And give strength to your bones; you will be like a watered garden, And like a spring of water whose waters do not fail." This verse is talking about the strength that Fasting gives to our spirit-man. The bones prophet Isaiah was referring to here are the bones of our spiritual life. Nothing draws us closer to God as Fasting and prayers combined with the word. These combinations are detrimental to the flesh and the Devil. The art of Fasting is lost to many believers today. We want a quick fix and five-point to deliverance. Ten-point on how to get rich quickly. Saints, to work in Holiness fasting is a must. The next verse speaks of more benefits that Fasting brings,

12. "And your people will rebuild the ancient ruins; You will raise up and restore the age-old foundations [of buildings that have been laid waste]; You will be called Repairer of the Breach,

Restorer of Streets with Dwellings

HOW TO PRACTICE THE FEAR OF GOD

Proverbs 10:27
The fear of the Lord prolongs life, but the years of the wicked will be shortened.

One of the leading causes of many death in the body today is the lack of fear of God in believers' lives. Many lives are cut short because they fell short. Some Christians talk and act without remorse, destroying the work of God with their mouth and actions. Speaking falsely against the work of God and the men/women of God without understanding the principle of "touch not". 2 Samuel 6:3-8 and 1 Chronicles 13:6-12 gave an account of a man call Uzza. He tried to protect the ark of God from falling; he thought he was helping and died as a consequence of trying to help God without God's endorsement. God struck him down for his assumption. We cannot help God as much as we try. Lack of spiritual insight can lead to spiritual malpractice.

Pray this Prayer: Lord help me to be spiritually sensitive.
The fear of the Lord is a work of the Holy Spirit, but it starts with inviting Him into your life and ask Him to help you practice the fear of the Lord. God, the Holy Spirit will not invite himself in your life without your permission. Now, I am well aware that we cannot spiritually govern ourselves without the Holy Spirit's inward work. Here are some scriptural foundations to help you increase the fear of God in you.

    a.   **Recognized that grace makes it possible** Ephesians 2:8-9 for by grace you have been saved through faith, and that not of yourselves; it <u>is the gift of God</u>, not of works, lest anyone should boast.

Acknowledge the work of grace that makes it possible for God to walk amongst men. It is by His grace we have been saved and not by our effort; we have no grounds for boasting. The finished work of Christ makes access to the father possible.
According to God's standard, no man is worthy to walk with God. The new covenant made it possible Bible says Colossians 1:20, and to reconcile all things to Himself, by Him, whether things on earth or things in heaven, having made peace through the blood of His cross. The main point you must press before God should be that Jesus Christ has died as the Mediator of

the new covenant. One of the benefits of that covenant "is God will write His law in your heart & put His fear into you." When you truly realize that it is not about your work but His finished work on the cross, I believe reverent fear will increase in you.

Pray this with me: Lord, by the blood of your son Jesus.

Put as much fear in my heart as warrants by the new covenant.

a. *Feed your spirit with Scriptures.*
Psalm 119:11 your Word I have hidden in my heart that I might not sin against you.

Eat the scriptures, Your words were found, and I ate them, And Your Word was to me the joy and rejoicing of my heart; For I am called by Your name, O Lord God of hosts. Jeremiah 15:16.

What is your spiritual diet? What you eat is who you are. You can't be filled with God and be full of the Devil. The two don't mix. It is like water and oil. John 1:5 light shines in the darkness, and the darkness cannot put it out. When you regularly fill your mind and spirit with the Word, you will begin to notice that you obey God naturally. Keep God's Word daily before you by studying and apply it throughout your whole day. It is a fact that when you keep something daily before you over time, it becomes part of you. Through the mutation of the Word in your heart, you will begin to grow in the reverent fear of God. You will be in awe of him.

b. Practice His Presence.

Practicing his Presence is vital to increase the fear of God in our hearts. The truth of the matter is you cannot obey a distant being. One of the reasons Jesus came down was and still is to bring us up to his level.

Ephesians 2:6 And God raised us up with Christ and seated us with him in the heavenly realms in Christ Jesus.

The reason he did that is to give us a position of authority and fellowship. Acknowledging Him in our daily activities can go a long way in increasing His reverend fear in our hearts. Doing things as simple as saying thank you, Jesus, throughout your day, Lord, I love you, etc. It helps in keeping Him front and center through your day. I do this throughout my day often, and it is life-changing. If God loves one thing, it is to be recognized and to be believed. Let no man lie to you just as you need his attention; he needs you too. You cannot be out of sync (Out of touch) and expect to gain His richness. Recognizing Him in our daily life is a life- transforming experience. May the Holy Spirit help us cultivate His Presence in Jesus' name. Amen!

c. Walk closely with those that walk in fear of God.
Proverbs 13:20 (MSG) Become wise by walking with the wise; hang out with fools and watch your life fall to pieces.

Everyone has the opportunity and right to choose their intimate friends. They have to be men and women who walk in fear of God. Scripture says in Proverbs 27:17 "iron sharpens iron". There is power in association and that is why scriptures admonish us not to associate with evil men/woman 2 Cor 6:14. The friends we keep determine the people we become. Whether we believe it or not, we learn from our associations. Their lives influence us. The powerful thing that I discovered from scriptures is our association/associates have a voice in the realms of spirit. God's

Word declares;

Malachi 3:16 Amplified "Then those who feared the Lord [with awe-filled reverence] spoke to one another, and the Lord paid attention and heard it, and a book of remembrance was written before Him of those who fear the Lord [with an attitude of reverence and respect] and who esteem His name." Wow! Those that fear God spoke and the Lord heard their voice. Friends choose your friends wisely because what they say and do affects you. If you desire to grow in the fear of God, associate yourself with those that fear God.

d. *Pray earnestly for an increase of the fear of God in you.*

Luke 18:1 pray consistently and never quit.

Prayer is the lifeblood of the believer. Pray is a kingdom principle; men/women must always pray without quitting. We are admonished in scriptures to ask, and we shall receive; seek, and we shall find and knock the door shall be open Matt 7:7. Bible declares; Ask anything in His name, and according to His will, he will do it. John 14:14 and 1 John 5:14 when we pray for the increase of the Lord's fear in us, He listens and answers. Why? Because it's according to His will for us. Begin to pray for its increase in you now.

In conclusion, when you begin to combine all these character builders' measured above, you will start to see the result. Over time you will become a better friend, better husband, or wife. A better CEO, better employee, a better employer, and overall a better person but, you have to choose to start today.

2

"Love is stronger than hate"

Break THE LIMIT

break the limits

Hate Or Love | 2

"Love is stronger than hate" Unknown.

Let's start with a quote from the Mini-series, John Adams. In one of the scenes, Paul GIAMATTI, who played Adams, expressed his frustration to his wife, Abagail, played by Laura Lainey, on how people misunderstood some of his words and good intentions.

He said: "My thoughts are so clear to me each one takes perfect shape within my mind, but when I speak when I offer them to others. They seem to lose all definition."

For some who do not know who John Adams was,

John Adams, not to be confused with his son John Quincy Adams, was an American statesman, attorney, diplomat, writer, and founding father who served as the second president of the United States from 1797 to 1801. John Adams was a very accomplished attorney even before he became president. Adams was a political activist before the revolution. Besides, he had many other accomplishments that are not mentioned in this book. He was still one of the most misunderstood and hated presidents in American history with all his accomplishments.

Johns Adams was devoted to the right of counsel and presumption of innocence. During the British rule of the American Colonies, the British treated the Americans as second-class citizens. Adam hated that despite his protest against the British treatment of the colonials. He defied the time's anti-British sentiment and successfully defended British soldiers against murder charges arising from the Boston Massacre. Here is what happened a small argument between British Private Hugh White and a few colonists outside the Custom House on King Street. The discussion began to escalate as more colonists gathered and began to harass and throw snowballs and sticks at Private White. Soon more colonists came to the scene as a result of the dispute. The local British officer of the watch, Captain Thomas Preston, sent some soldiers over to the Custom House to contain the situation.
However, the sight of British soldiers armed with bayonets just exasperated the crowd further. They

began to shout at the soldiers, daring them to shoot at them.
Captain Preston then arrived and tried to get the group to disperse. Unfortunately, someone in the crowd threw an object that's struck one of the soldiers, Private Montgomery, and knocked him down. He fired into the crowd, according to him, in self-defense. After a few seconds of stunned silence, some soldiers fired into the crowd as well. Three colonists died immediately, and two more died later from bullet wounds.

The British government wanted the soldiers to have a fair trial, but no lawyer wanted to take their case. John Adams stepped up and defended the soldiers. He argued that the soldier had the right to protect themselves against the mob. He demonstrated that the soldiers thought their lives were in danger and had to defend themselves. Six of the eight soldiers were found not- guilty, and two were found guilty of manslaughter.

Despite Adams's personal feelings toward the British, he followed the evidence. You can tell the character of a man by the way he treats people and how he disagrees with others, disallowing his personal feelings to get in the way of doing the right thing. Many of us today should not let our emotions get in the way of sound judgment.
Especially in the climate that we live in now, when we disagree with someone, we paint them black. He is one of

my favorite presidents. He was a very complex man, and so he was misunderstood by many American historians. Despite his flaws, one thing is sure: Adams loved his country, and he was good at heart. Many called him naive and unpatriotic because he defended people he disagrees with; others say he was over-ambitious, but I call that passionate. Some say he was very opinionated, but I call that principled. God made us in different shades, sizes, and shapes. If all of us were the same, life would be boring and uneventful.

John Adams was a flawed man, just like many of us. He made some mistakes just like many of us have done. The Scripture says, "We all stumble in many ways. Anyone who is never at fault in what they say is perfect, able to keep their whole body in check (James 3:2). Sometimes hate or hatred is a result of misunderstanding a person's personality or point of view.

WHAT IS HATE AND WHAT ARE THE SOURCES OF HATE?

Hate is a human emotion; it is defned as an intense or passionate dislike for someone or something, etc.

Sigmund Freud defined "hate as an ego state that wishes to destroy the source of its unhappiness. "With hate on the rise, one would wonder why?

Let us discuss some of the sources of hate:

1. **FEAR:** We fear people or things we don't understand. The same God created us; we breathe the same oxygen just like the next woman or man. Despite our unique culture or upbringing, we all bleed red. We belong to the same family, the human family.

We are born into the world. We grow up, we love, and we get old and die. We differ in beliefs and opinions, but the most significant difference between us

humans is the skin tone. We all feel pain. Sometimes when we face people or things that make us fear, through open dialogue, we suddenly realize that the things or people that we saw as monsters were not monsters at all.

2. **IGNORANCE:** Sometimes people hate because they are ignorant of the person they hate. Sometimes, lack of information or the proper knowledge about an individual or thing can be a determining factor for hate. For instance, a person receives a piece of information that his neighbor hates him.

Upon receiving that information, the recipient refuses to ascertain whether the story is true or false. He or she begins to show hate towards that individual based on unverified information. He starts saying things like, "I do not like him because he hates me." He/she had no verified facts to prove his/her point. I have discovered that many times information gets distorted as it travels from one person to the next. In my experience, people were not as others portrayed them. Just a gap in the information or lack of communication can be a source of hate. Suppose we can set aside the time to verify information concerning many things. In that case, we will save many relationships and communities.

3.   NURTURE: Some are brainwashed to hate certain group or groups of people because they are unique. One of the disservice people can do to this world is to tell a lie about people or groups to an innocent mind. Have that person believe that the lie that was said to him/her is the truth and use the lie that's taught to him/her to hate on a people or a group. It is disturbing! Hate can take a severe toll on the mind. Its effect on the human psyche can be devastating. Martin Luther King, Jr once said I paraphrase "Hate begets hate; we must meet the forces of hate with the power of love..." Hatred is unhealthy for both the hater and the one hate is directed at.

HOW CAN WE OVERCOME HATE?

Scriptures give us some insight:

Song of Solomon 8:6 "Place me like a seal over your heart, like a seal on your arm; for Love is as strong as death.

I John 4:7-12 NKJV

7. Beloved, let us love one another, for Love is of God, and everyone who loves is born of God and knows God.

8. He who does not love does not know God, for God is Love.

9. In this, the Love of God was manifested toward us that God has sent His only begotten Son into the world that we might live through Him

10. In this is Love, not that we loved God, but that He loved us and sent His Son to be the propitiation for our sins.

11. Beloved, if God so loved us, we also ought to love one another.

12. No one has seen God at any time. If we love one another, God abides in us, and His Love has been perfected in us."

Verse 7 lets us love one another, for Love is of God, and everyone who loves is born of God and knows God.

Another translation says for "love comes from God". Everyone who loves has been born of God and knows God.

From the above scriptures, we can conclude that Love is the antidote for hate or hatred.

In Romans 12:21, "Do not be overcome by evil, but overcome evil with good." You cannot put out the fire by using fire that happens when someone hates you, and you hate the person; in return, Mohandas Gandhi said, "An eye for an eye will make the whole world blind."

WE SHOULD SEEK TO UNDERSTAND OTHERS.

Johns Adams was a unique man. An anomaly; therefore, he has often been misinterpreted even God invites us to understand him Isaiah 1:18 "come now let reason together..."

To gain a clear perspective on people. We should find out why they act the way they do; then maybe we can approach them from a place of understanding.

WE SHOULD CELEBRATE OUR DIFFERENCES INSTEAD OF FEAR THEM.

The United States was founded on the premise of the celebration of differences. Therefore, all people should be treated as equal: Blacks, whites, Africans, Americans, Asians, etc. We may have different cultures, but we are all humans.

WE MUST MAKE ROOM FOR DIALOGUE INSTEAD OF CONTENTION.

Many of the things we argue about, if we take a closer look, sometimes are irrelevant. We will not know that if we refuse dialogue, we will keep on hating on others. The voice telling you that everyone hates you is the Devil; don't listen to him. Reach out to your brother or sister. It not always easy to reach out to some people, especially complicated people, but that should not stop us from reaching out as an act of Love. Jesus was a master of outreach. He gave opportunity even to those he disagreed with. We are called to make peace, not contention.

2 Corinthians 5:18-19

"God is love," the scriptures say. There is no rationale for hate! No matter your reason or reasons for hating your brother or sister, that reason is not good enough. It's unhealthy for you and the person you are directing your hatred to. It's ok to have differences of opinion but, it's never ok, to hate someone for being different.

Racism

Racism has been the source of many calamities in history"

03

Break THE LIMITS

WORLD ISSUES

Racism

03

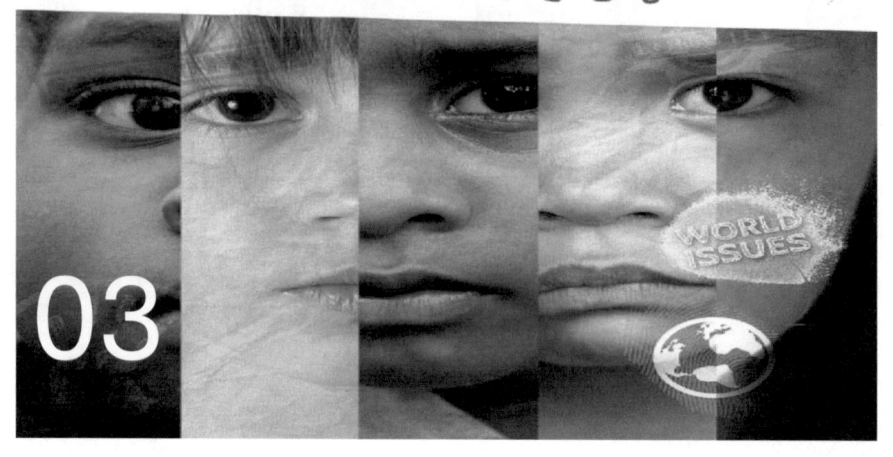

Genesis 1:26-27 Amplified Bible, Classic Edition. "God said, Let Us [Father, Son, and Holy Spirit] make mankind in Our image, after Our likeness, and let them have complete authority over the fish of the sea, the birds of the air, the [tame] beasts, and over all of the earth, and over everything that creeps upon the earth. So God created man in His image, in the image and likeness of God He created him; male and female He created them"

Galatians 3:27-28 King James Version
"For as many of you as have been baptized into Christ have put on Christ. There is neither Jew nor Greek, there is neither bond nor free, there is neither male nor female: for ye are all one in Christ Jesus."

Galatians 3:27-28 Amplified Bible, Classic Edition
For as many [of you], as were baptized into Christ [into a spiritual union and communion with Christ, the Anointed One, the Messiah], have put on (clothed yourselves with) Christ.

There is [now no distinction] neither Jew nor Greek, there is neither slave nor free, there is not male and female; for you are all one in Christ Jesus.

To understand discrimination or racial bias we must first deal with its root cause. Now, let me stop and insert this my intention in this chapter is not to offend anyone or downplay certain aspects of our collective human civilization. Rather is to give us a biblical perspective on racism and suggestions on how to help move the conversation and solution further. I believe that the root cause of racism lies deep in man's nature, wounded and bruised by original sin Romans 3:23 puts this in the best way For all have sinned, and come short of the glory of God;

What is racism?

Racism is the belief that some races are inherently superior or inferior to others, leading to discrimination and prejudice based on race. Racism has been the source of many calamities in history including the Nazi brutal murder of 6.3 million Jews which was over 60% of their Jews population. Racist people & institutionalized racism did that.

Racism was the reason why King Leopold after convincing the major powers of his day to recognize a huge part of central Africa as his personal property. He called it État Indépendant du Congo, the Congo Free State. It was the world's only private colony, and Leopold referred to himself as its "proprietor." He went ahead to savagery murdering ten million Congolese Africans because to him they were expendable racism.

Racism was the reason for the Era of segregation in the United States. Jim Crow laws were a byproduct of racism. What are Jim Crow Laws: Jim Crow laws were a collection of state and local statutes that legalized racial segregation. It was named after a Black minstrel show character, it's existed for close to 100 years, from the post- Civil War era until 1968. Though the Civil Rights Act was passed in 1964. Jim Crow laws were meant to marginalize black Americans by denying them the right to vote, hold jobs, get an education, or other opportunities. Those who attempted to defy such laws were often faced with arrest, fines, jail sentences, violence, and death.

America and the West have a long history of discrimination based on race and gender though considerable effort has been made to dismantle racism in America by passing swiping legislation to combat the spread of this sickness called racism. Such as the Civil Rights Act of 1964 which made it illegal to discriminate against a person based on his/her race, color, religion, sex, and national origin. Though great progress has been made more can be done to further the human cause.

As the scriptures stated above all men/women are created in the image of God, and therefore all races and ethnic groups have the same equal status, unique value, and dignity before GOD. Christ emphasized loving one's neighbor as oneself and treating others with kindness, regardless of their race or ethnicity. No true Christian can condone or entertain racism or racist acts because the scriptures are clear on racism and is this; God doesn't approve of it.

Mark 12:30-31 Jesus said,
"The first in importance is, 'Listen, Israel: The Lord your God is one; so love the Lord God with all your passion and prayer and intelligence and energy.' And here is the second: 'Love others as well as you love yourself.' There is no other commandment that ranks with these."

Leviticus 19:18
"Don't seek revenge or carry a grudge against any of your people. Love your neighbor as yourself. I am God."

Matthew 19:18-19
The man asked, "What in particular?" Jesus said, "Don't murder, don't commit adultery, don't steal, don't lie, honor your father and mother, and love your neighbor as you do yourself."

Luke 10:27 He said,

"That you love the Lord your God with all your passion and prayer and muscle and intelligence—and that you love your neighbor as well as you do yourself."

This is gospel truth, despite the bad press that the church has had and still getting, no true follower of the teachings of Christ can be a racist. Even if he/she started as one give them time in the word, prayers, and fellowship with faithful believers their perspective will change for the better.

2 Corinthians 3:18 Amplified Bible, Classic Edition
"And all of us, as with unveiled face, [because we] continued to behold [in the Word of God] as in a mirror the glory of the Lord, are constantly being transfigured into His very own image in ever increasing splendor and from one degree of glory to another; [for this comes] from the Lord [Who is] the Spirit."

What that means in this context is this: When you interact with The Word of God through reading, studying, listening and even preaching it has in its DNA the ability to transform you into your glorious status, from better and better than only the spirit of God can accomplish. The scriptures command us to love one another. He also tells us that we are not of God, if we do not love one another. Racism has no hiding place in the heart and character of a Spirit-filled, born-again Christian that's the absolute truth period.

1 John 4:8 Amplified Bible, Classic Edition
"He who does not love has not become acquainted with God [does not and never did know Him], for God is love."

Jesus Christ was very clear on racism. He was a Jew, a Middle Eastern and He interacted with a centurion/Roman captain who was a Caucasian/white that was new in his days a rabbi interacting with a Gentile/Non-Jewish? According to the Jewish sentiment that was not supposed to happen but it did in Matthew 8:5-13. Jesus didn't only interact with him; he offered to come to his house and help which was forbidden.

The Bible says thus in Matthew 8:5-8
"As Jesus went into Capernaum, a centurion came up to Him, begging Him,6 And saying, Lord, my servant boy is lying at the house paralyzed and distressed with intense pains. And Jesus said to him, I will come and restore him.8 But the centurion replied to Him, Lord, I am not worthy or fit to have You come under my roof; but only speak the word, and my servant boy will be cured."

In addition, The Lord Jesus also interacted with Africans for example the man who carried his cross was Simeon of Cyrene. Cyrene was a Greek city in the province of Cyrenaica, in eastern Libya, in northern Africa. Christ is the convergence of race, color, rich and poor. There is neither poor nor rich, Jews or Gentiles we are all one in Christ Jesus. Galatians 3:28 points this out its stated: There is [now no distinction] neither Jew nor Greek, there is neither slave nor free, there is not male and female; for you are all one in Christ Jesus.

HOW CAN WE SOLVE RACISM IN AMERICA AND THE WORLD?

As we stated earlier the root cause of racism lies deep in man's falling nature, wounded and bruised by original sin Romans 3:23 put this in the best way For all have sinned, and come short of the glory of God; I am a realist I don't believe that racism can be completely eradicated in this realm. There will always be people who are racist that is a fact. However, there are steps we can take to dismantle racism. It starts with you. Like we stated earlier man's "sinful nature" aided by learned behavior
is the root cause of racism. Learning behavior can be traced back to the original sin. That's been said the first step to dismantle racism is to truly be born again.

Now, I know some in the West are apprehensive about Christianity because of some of the past sins or negative experiences they have or may not have had. Please allow me to say this everyone has some form of bias. What do I mean? First, let's define bias What is bias? the Britannica Dictionary defines bias as "a tendency to believe that some people, ideas, etc., are better than others that usually results in treating some people unfairly." there are many forms or types of bias but one that is appropriate for this topic is implicit bias or implicit stereotype a term coined by psychologists Mahzarin Benaji and Anthony Greenwald.

Implicit bias, also known as implicit prejudice or implicit attitude, is a negative attitude, of which one is not consciously aware, against a specific social group. It's shaped by our experience and learned associates or behavior. In scripture, Peter was an example of someone with implicit bias. At one point in his ministry, he was biased toward the Gentiles because of his Jewish upbringing. Apostle Paul confronted him on that. Galatians 2:11-13

"But when Peter came to Antioch, I had to oppose him to his face, for what he did was very wrong. When he first arrived, he ate with the Gentile believers, who were not circumcised. But afterward, when some friends of James came, Peter wouldn't eat with the Gentiles anymore. He was afraid of criticism from these people who insisted on the necessity of circumcision. As a result, other Jewish believers followed Peter's hypocrisy, and even Barnabas was led astray by their hypocrisy."

Bias becomes institutional racism when it becomes institutionalized, philosophized as it was before it was outlawed in 1964. Implicit bias turns into racism when left unchecked by the individual. Implicit bias is shaped by experience and based on one's learned associations between particular qualities and social categories, including race and/or gender. Individuals' perceptions and behaviors can be influenced by the implicit biases they hold, even if they are unaware they hold such biases. Implicit bias is an aspect of implicit social cognition: the phenomenon that perceptions, attitudes, and stereotypes can operate before conscious intention or endorsement. There is no measure of racism in scripture because God the author of the scriptures doesn't believe in different races, He believes in only one race that's the human race.

Acts 17:26 states it like this *"And hath made of one blood all nations of men for to dwell on all the face of the earth..."* he has made of one" Galatians 2:11-13 Paul Confronts Peter on his bias against the Gentiles

"But when Peter came to Antioch, I had to oppose him to his face, for what he did was very wrong. When he first arrived, he ate with the Gentile believers, who were not circumcised. But afterward, when some friends of James came, Peter wouldn't eat with the Gentiles anymore. He was afraid of criticism from these people who insisted on the necessity of circumcision. As a result, other Jewish believers followed Peter's hypocrisy, and even Barnabas was led astray by their hypocrisy."

SOLUTION

To address racism, the bible teaches us to encourage followers to challenge their prejudices, actively promote equality and justice, and pursue reconciliation and unity. This can be achieved through actions such as advocating for equal rights, engaging in intercultural dialogue, fostering inclusive communities, and working towards dismantling systemic injustices. Ultimately, solving racism requires a collective effort from individuals, communities, and institutions to promote understanding, empathy, and respect for all people, as guided by biblical principles. From a biblical perspective, solving racism involves understanding and applying the principles that we stated earlier. The principle of love, equality, and justice for all. I believe solving any form of discrimination requires addressing systemic issues, promoting education and awareness, and working towards creating equal opportunities for all individuals. Emphasizing empathy, and compassion, and recognizing the shared humanity among people can help bridge divides and foster a more inclusive society.

It's important to approach this conversation about discrimination with sensitivity and a willingness to listen and learn from others' experiences. By actively promoting equality, justice, and understanding, we can contribute to reducing discrimination and creating a more inclusive world.

REVERSE RACISM

Now, we cannot close this chapter without addressing the current state of society, especially in the West. While great stride has been made in the effort to stamp out racism. This plague I believe is making a comeback in another form. It's called Reverse racism.

Reverse racism is a term often used to describe situations where blacks who were historically marginalized groups exhibit prejudice or discrimination against whites who were historically privileged groups. However, it's important to note that the concept of reverse racism is contentious, as it suggests a power dynamic that may not align with the historical and systemic context of racism.

However, to address any form of discrimination or prejudice, including perceived instances of reverse racism, it is essential to promote equality, understanding, and empathy. This involves fostering open dialogue and creating inclusive spaces where individuals from diverse backgrounds can share their experiences and perspectives. The fact of the matter is not every white enjoyed this I quote "privilege class" There were whites that were as poor or poorer than some blacks. In other words, they share the same destiny. Friends, we are stronger together than apart.

We must not replace evil with another kind of evil it's wrong on all levels. In the words of Dr. Martin Luther King: "Injustice anywhere is a threat to justice everywhere. We are caught in an inescapable network of mutuality, tied in a single garment of destiny. Whatever affects one directly, affects all indirectly.
We must resist the temptation of replacing discrimination with another form of discrimination. We are better than this. Romans 12:21 tells us that: *Be not overcome of evil, but overcome evil with good.*

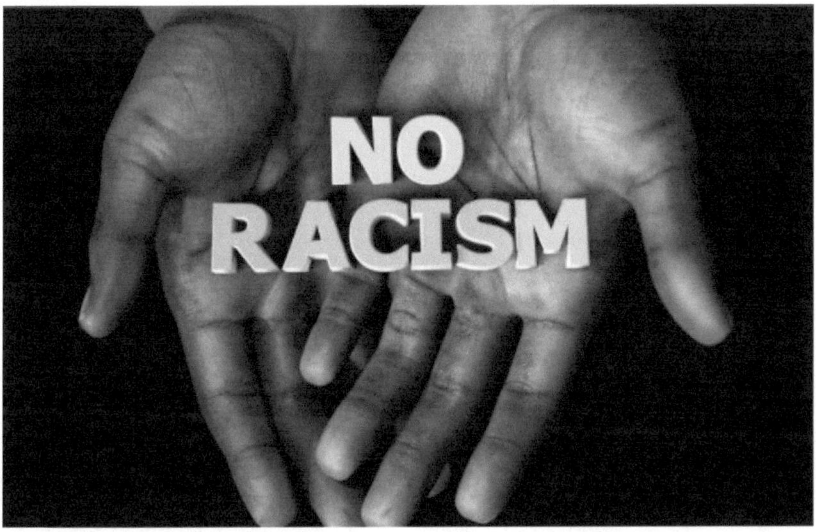
NO
RACISM

A fulfilled or accomplished life cannot happen by wishing

4

▶ Break THE LIMIT

breakthelimit

HOW TO LIVE A FULFILLED LIFE | 04

I believe everyone wishes and desires to live a fulfilled life, but very few do. Why? Because things do not happen on their own. Someone must make it happen.

There must be an initiator. Through my continuing studies of successful people, I have discovered that there are natural sequences that culminate in the desired lifestyle. It is a fact that everyone loves the feeling of accomplishment. At a certain point in our lives; we want to look back at our life and say wow!! I had a good run. I am truly satisfied with my life. I believe it is an innate desire of the human race. We love the sense of accomplishment. We want to live a life of accomplishments but, a fulfilled or accomplished life cannot happen by wishing it into existence. It takes a conscious effort If we must live a fulfilled life.

In this chapter, we will examine some practical steps to living a fulfilled life.

1.   KNOW YOUR BOUNDARIES AND STICK TO THEM.

Now, if you are familiar with my person, you might have heard me say things like God Created us in Christ without limits. That is true in many contexts. It is also true that we have boundaries or limits. Job 14:5 A person's days are determined; you have decreed the number of his months and have set limits he cannot exceed." Even freedom has its limit. If no regulation constitutes freedom, crime will be more rampant. That said: let's use something basic for instance, your unlimited mobile date is truly not so unlimited. Now, this is true about unlimited data plans; there are no limits to the amount of data you can use. There are, however, very truly limits to data speed. When you are buying an unlimited plan, you might find language that resembles this: Customers may experience reduced speeds at certain network congestion times. They are basically saying: If our network gets busy, we might slow you down, or the Customer may experience reduced speeds after 30GB of usage. What's that saying: If you use too much of your data, we'll probably slow you down.

When we start stepping out of our limitations we end up in a mess. Boundaries in some cases are for our good. Therefore, sometimes it is essential to adhere to them.

2. DISCOVER YOUR PURPOSE AND LIVE IT.

Everyone has two birthdays the day you were born and the day you discover your purpose. Age is not the function of time, it's a function of discovery of one's purpose.

Hebrews 11:24 "By faith Moses, when he had grown up, refused to be called the son of Pharaoh's daughter,"

Your purpose is that thing you were born to do, that problem you were engineered to solve. The discovery of one's purpose is the start of life. Purpose gives you passion, and passion creates results. Speaking of passion, Albert Einstein was one of the greatest minds of the 20th century. Albert's father wanted him to study electrical engineering, but he disliked that field. He had a passion for math and physics from a very young age. He excelled at both subjects. He later became a theoretical physicist who developed relativity theory, a significant pillar in modern physics. If he had not discovered his purpose, we might never know him. YOU CAN ONLY MAKE A MARK IN YOUR PURPOSE. PURPOSE FULFILLED CREATES LEGACY. He lived his purpose. Therefore, discover your purpose and live it!

HOW TO DISCOVER YOUR PURPOSE

As far as purpose is concerned, there is one word I believe you are familiar with; the term is "talent" Everyone has it, but few fully explore it. Others think they don't have any. Those who believe they do never reach their peak performance. Let me say this for those who do not know they have talent; you are talented! You have an anointing from God in your life. Now, we will be using words like talent, gift, gifting, assignment, and anointing interchangeably in this chapter's context.

These are words we will use to describe "purpose."

Let's take a look at Genesis 1:1 and Genesis 1:27.

Genesis 1:1 in the beginning, God created the heavens and the earth. Verse 27 so God created man in his image, in the image of God created he him; male and female created he them.

These verses of scriptures debunked the idea of a talentless individual. Genesis 1:1 tells us three things. 1. There was a beginning, 2. There is a creator, and 3. He created. Verse 27 tells us that he "created man in His image" God is the creator and He made you in His image/picture, that means your primary gift amongst many is creativity, though some more than others as the parable of the talents suggested Matt 25:14-30. Everyone has a God-given talent/gift, but your talent is your potential. Meaning it requires discovery and development. Many never discover the purpose for existence; I believe 90% of all people never reach their full potential. Few reached it, and even fewer maximum their God-given gift. When you function in your gifting
or anointing, you have no rival.

3. INDICATOR OR POINTER TO YOUR PURPOSE

What is that thing that moves you amongst all others? When you close your eyes, what do you see yourself enjoy doing? What do you love? What is that thing that others struggled to accomplish? You do the same thing flawlessly. What gives you a burden? That's an indicator/pointer to your purpose. Talent is your potential, your inherent ability or capacity.

Maybe when you were growing up, you love to read and write; you admire writers. Writing moves you.

You love the library and Books make you happy. There may be a writer in you. Maybe you start singing at a very early age. Others had to train their voice, stick to strict protocols like not drinking cold water, etc. while in your case, you probably break all the voice training rules: you drink cold water at will and still sing effortlessly. That is an indicator of your purpose. A childhood Pain that turns into passion and passion became a purpose. Your purpose is that thing you are engineered to do, the problem God created you to solve. Your purpose is the environment you are gifted to impact.

For example, take a fish out of the water and put it on dry land; it will gasp for air. Take that same fish and put it in water; it will swim beautifully. Why? Because water is the environment fish was created to operate in. its genius emerges in water. You can only make a real impact in your place of assignment. You are struggling today. The reason may be you are not in your area of assignment. You are frustrated with your chosen field; you are never happy with your Job you are constantly feeling burnt out. Perhaps that is because you are not in your place of assignment. Strength and satisfaction are available only in your area of assignment. Friends, you were made to function in a specific location.

I have a medical doctor at home, and she can tell you that she fell in love with medicine at an early age. She knew she could only be happy practicing that which she was created to do. Since the first day I got saved as a teenager, I knew that I was called into ministry, despite knowing I was running from the lime-light (Public life). I did everything to exclude myself, but it never worked out until I accepted my call. Friends, discovering your purpose is the start of life. Purpose gives you passion, and passion creates results.

Albert Einstein, as measured above, could not have functioned well outside of the sciences. His impact would have been minimal at best. Purpose gives your fulfillment; you hate your Job because it is not your purpose. When you are doing what you were born to do, it does not feel like a job. Your purpose is your work, that thing you take pleasure in, which gives you the greatest fulfillment.

LIVE WITH AN OPEN HEART AND MIND, EVEN IF IT HURTS.

Love as a verb is one of the strongest emotions. When you decide to live with an open heart some will abuse you. Be careful of those but, do not be afraid to love. Yes, some may even hurt you a few times. That's shouldn't make you lose your love for people. When you decide to live a life of love, it has its advantages and some disadvantage but, its rewards are endless.

You are a product of God's love. John 3:16" for God so loved the world that he gave..." Romans 5:8 God demonstrates his love for us in this: While we were still sinners, Christ died for us." Some of the most abused individuals today are men and women with loving hearts. People may call you names and tried to label you etc. They did the same to Jesus Christ. The Pharisees and Sadducees called Jesus a friend of the tax collectors and sinners but, that's didn't stop him from reaching out to the least of these.

Do not rush to judgment. Have an open heart and mind. Be accepting of others. Love people for who they are, not for what you can get from them, and your open heart and hands will win them over.

STOP POSTPONING WHAT YOU MUST DO TODAY.

Stop putting away things you should accomplish today for tomorrow. There are no guarantees in life. The only assurance we have is in Christ. It's a fact that challenges are never going to be over. They are part of life. So deal with them. Life's challenges are one of the constants in life. Stop waiting for the good times. I want to challenge you from now on, spend at least an hour doing that thing you will love to do if you were financially secure. Stop postponing what you must do today because you lack creative discipline. The future is now, activate it!

Proverbs 24:27 "[Put first things first.] Prepare your work outside and get it ready for yourself in the field, and afterward build your house and establish a home." it's said that a journey of a thousand miles begins with a step. Start making moves now that will help enhance and secure your future. Let me give you a piece of advice.

Please listen to me: Stop trying to fix everyone and lose focus on yourself. You are the most important person in the world and you deserve a break too. Listen, if you were the only person on earth, Christ would have still died for you. In conclusion, do what you must do now! So that you may live the life that you deserve tomorrow.

6. NEVER SACRIFICE YOUR INTEGRITY FOR PERSONAL GAIN.

What is Integrity? I define Integrity as the quality of being whole, having strong moral principles. Integrity came from the Latin word integer. Integer means whole or complete 99.99% of anything is not 100%... Principles are the foundation of any lasting productive life. Those that cut corners always end up being cut down. God may bypass protocol to favour you but he will not bypass the process. There is no shortcut or quick fix to life neither is it one size fits all. There is no right way of doing the wrong things. Anything or anyone that causes a person to compromise his/her principles consistently will eventually destroy that person. Look at what happened recently to a much respected Hollywood film producer. He sacrificed his Integrity for personal craving, and it cost him his freedom. Most people that have a public moral falling watch their life closely, it did not happen the day it was discovered. It happened over time.

Anything or anyone that gradually chips on a person's moral standing will eventually destroy him/her. Principles produce principal life. Receive grace to live above falling in the mighty name of Jesus.

7. DON'T USE YOUR CHALLENGE AS A EXCUSE

I recently watched an inspirational video of a young wrestler and a great athlete. This youngster has won many championships. He has competed in major tournaments across the country and has always been victorious. In every sport that he has ever engaged in, he has always come out on top. If I can summarize his athletic ability by two words, those words will be "incredible and magnificent". Yeah! Those are heavy words you get the point. Right about now, you may be saying to yourself, Paul, there are lots of incredible athletes in America. As a matter of fact, around the world that my friend, you are right but, I left out some critical things in this story. Did I tell you that he is a young adult that was born without limbs? I can hear you saying to yourself maybe it is Special Olympics. Nope! All the competitions he competed in were not Special Olympics but just regular tournaments with regular people.

He did not let his challenge became an excuse. As I was watching it, it dawned on me that THERE IS ABILITY IN DISABILITY. Question? What is that excuse that you been using? What is that crutch that you been carrying all this while? Oh, Mr. Paul, you don't understand in this country, people like us are at a disadvantage. Bishop David Oyedepo, a man of God

I admire very much, made a profound statement. I quote, "there is no mountain anywhere. Every man's ignorance is his mountain" end of quote. If you must fulfill destiny, you must throw away all your excuses. Sometimes back I preached a message titled "turning your excuses into uses" I outlined three main things that excuses does to an individual: (1) Causes one to lose their true identity

(2) You relinquish your power (3) you chip away part of yourself. I believe strongly that any negative situation can become helpful. Depending on how you handle it. Make an effort to stop using your challenge as an excuse.

LISTEN TO YOUR FRIENDS, LEARN FROM YOUR CRITICS

Everyone has something to teach us if only we are listening. True friends always have your back. Listen to them take their observations on things make changes when necessary. On critics lets me establish a fact.
CRITICS AND THEIR CRITICISMS ARE PART OF THE
NATURAL CIRCLE OF LIFE. In this day and age, we live there is no shortage of them. You can let them get under your skin or you can put their criticism to good use.

Let me tell you a true story. A certain bishop told us a story about a colleague that used to be a thorn in his flesh every time this man will preach offensive things about him. If he did an anointing service today this man will go on TV the next day blast the bishop. Saying, "some people are abusing the use of the anointing oil that is not the way the Bible says it must be utilized", etc. This critic says things to undermine the bishop's honest work. He did this for years; one faithful day, he and the bishop met at the Lagos airport; he thought the bishop would go off on him. The bishop walked up to him and shook his hand. The bishop said thank you for doing a wonderful job and the bishop went his way. The man stood there looking dumbfounded. Afterward, he left; the bishop said to his team I learned from that man not to do what he

is saying. Today the man of God that was critiquing this bishop has faded away but, the bishop ministry is growing forever relevant. I have discovered that life is a university; every day is a class. Class is in session. Question: which semester are you in?

5

We must not be satisfied
with the ordinary,
We should never accept mediocrity.

▶ Break THE LIMIT

Personal Growth — 05
break the limits

Philippians 3:13 Paul writes Brothers, "I do not consider that I have made it my own. But one thing I do: forgetting what lies behind and straining forward to what lies ahead."

Paul says to us in the above scripture that there should always be room for growth despite our height. We must always make room for more improvement in our attitude, perspective, finances, ministry, marriage, career, or whatever our hand finds to do. We must not be satisfied with the ordinary. We should never accept mediocrity. Acceptance of mediocrity makes a mediocre life.

Mind you; Apostle Paul was an accomplished man even before his conversion. After his conversion, he went all-in with his newfound faith. The Apostle applied himself more than all his colleagues; Paul was a man with an unbridled passion for excellence. He did not accept mediocrity. His mission in life was to bring the gospel to the gentiles. He worked tirelessly to accomplish the task. Apostle Paul refused to accept that he has apprehended. During his lifetime, he got to a point the scriptures recorded that he evangelized the known world. God called us to impact our world, but we must constantly upgrade ourselves to do that. We must grow daily. Growth or development for our species is an absolute necessity; it is part of the human life cycle. We were born into this world. We grow from a child to a teenager, from a teenager to a young adult. From young adults to adults, biological changes are natural to life from an adult to old age. So also is personal growth; it's necessary to grow in all aspects of life if we are to thrive, besides the few things we mentioned earlier.

WHY GROW?

Because that just what living things do. Living things grow. We, therefore, have two choices in life we either grow or die from lack of growth. If that what we must do to survive then, it means we have the capacity or potential for growth, but the potential is a possibility. We have to tap into that possibility by deliberately setting growth goals. Why grow? You may not know what you are fully capable of achieving until you set a course and pursue it. We as a species have unlimited growth potential. There are several mistakes I have observed we make about personal growth.

1. Refusal to Upgrade:

Because of advancement in technology and breakthroughs in sciences, professional in those fields are required to constantly go through a periodic upgrade in other to meet the demands of their respective industries; for instance, in the medical field, young doctors are required to retake an arduous exam every 7 to 10years to keep their credentials there is also an additional law that requires physicians of all ages to complete a complex set of requirements every two to three years.

Another example, pilot; after getting a bachelor's degree in aeronautical engineering, aircraft operations, aviation, or a related field, they must complete two months of ground training and need more than 1,600hours of flight experience. In addition to that, there is yearly training for airline pilots. They are tested in nine different areas every six months. Pilots must go into the simulator to practice emergency procedures while being assessed by an examiner over a couple of days.

Now, that is with those professionals and many others. You can apply this same principle of constant upgrade to your personal life. Which part of your life needs an upgrade? Do not just toss it aside say, oh! "I do not have time to work on it." I hear people make excuses for the improvement they are supposed to make. I hear people use words like, "my schedule is full. I have no time for this, nor for that, etc."

What is that area you need to grow? Is it your anger? There are anger management classes you can enroll in to help you combat that excessive anger. Scriptures,

Prayers, fasting & counseling can help as well. Your relationship with your wife, kids, loved ones, etc. is not improving? Get some professional help. Were you trying to get a job? Didn't you meet the requirements? Because of that, your application was rejected? Get more training and reapply! Do what will bring you up to speed on your chosen career. You are not paid for your smiles except you are in the service industry; you are paid for the value you bring. Upgrade to become an invaluable and irreplaceable asset.

HINDRANCE TO GROWTH.

ASSUMPTION: One of the biggest hindrances to growth is an assumption. As a pastor, I have the distinct honor and opportunity to mentor and counsel people I hear most exciting things. There was this particular fellow that came to me asking for my help with his relationship.

He said, pastor, pray for me this challenge I am going through; I need your prayers. I said, really? He said yes, sir, and then I asked him to explain, and he began to narrate the story. From his explanation, I got to find out that his problem did not need prayers alone. Coupled with prayers, he needed to make some lifestyle changes, and I gave him an assignment. I said to him, do these things. I believe your problem will be over. He said, ok, thank you, sir, and I prayed with him, and he left. Two weeks later, I called to check on his progress. I asked him if he did what we discussed. He said, no, pastor, I believe I am praying, and you have prayed for me that day everything will be fine. Then I replied? I said, if I heard you right, you did not do what I counseled you about you are using prayer as a crutch? I said nice talking with you later.

A few months later, I heard that he was back at it again. Now, don't get me wrong, I believe in pray and love to pray. I am in a praying ministry, but prayers cannot substitute principles as powerful as it is.

The assumption is a killer of great men. The brother refuses to combine prayers with principles. He assumed that since he has pray that will take care of all things. To assume is to be consumed. He refuses to grow up.

Growth will not happen by assumptions. Going to school getting a formal education is a start education continues after you hang up that gown, had the graduation party, etc. Most people have not read a book since they graduated. Others assume that as they grow older, they will ultimately succeed in other aspects of their life that assumption is further from the truth. Age is the length of time you have lived. It not a sign of personal growth. Growth mentally, financially, etc., requires an extra effort on your part.

Growth must be deliberate, and it must be intentional. Others assume that circumstances will teach them stuff but, the results are not always positive. There are some temptations or difficulties you go through that can change you for the worst. Do not live your growth to time and chance. That is not the way God intended for you to live. You are a deliberate creation. You did not happen by a biological accident despite the event that brought you here. If you must grow, stop the assumptions; growth must be intentional.

THINGS YOU SHOULD DO ABOUT GROWTH

COMMIT TO GROW DAILY.

Daily growth takes time; take time each day to focus on your personal development. I will suggest you start with 30minutes to an hour or more daily. Focus on that part of your life that you are having challenges. Draw up a plan to overcome the obstacles; for example, if your focus is spirituality, you want to get close to God, Set aside time for fellowship with him, study the scriptures, meditation, etc. It can be a particular time of the day or night. When the time comes, you have set aside. Stop everything you are doing and work on the things you had planned. Always keep that schedule. If it midnight prayers or 5 pm study, stick with it. You may fail a few times as you attempt to establish the schedule. Please don't give up stay with it over time; it will become an established schedule. In addition, ask the Holy Ghost for help. He is willing and ready to aid you in your pursue, engage Him.

BE CONSISTENT

What I mean by that is, don't do it today, and the next day you stop and pick up a month after. It said that "the secret of success lies in your daily routine" WHAT YOU DO DAILY DETERMINE, WHO YOU BECOME TOMORROW.

Your greatest adversary is not the devil, your most significant obstacle is not people, your biggest adversary, and the most critical obstacle is your flesh. Overcome it, and you will become that person.

Discipline

the ability to pursue what is right despite temptations to abandon it.

Break THE LIMITS

06

SELF DISCIPLINE

"I have fought the good fight, I have finished the race, and I have remained faithful."

2 Timothy 4:7 NLT

"All athletes are disciplined in their training... 1 Corinthians 9:25 NLT

The online dictionary defines self-discipline as "The ability to control one's feelings and overcome one's weaknesses; the ability to pursue what is right despite temptations to abandon it. Anything worthwhile demands a focus, and it requires discipline.

One of the greatest athletes of all time, Michael Jordan, practiced at least 8 hours daily. When he was in high school, he practiced so much that they had to kick him out of the gym. If not, he would not stop.

The most decorated Olympian, Michael Phelps, swims a minimum of 80,000 meters a week at peak training phases, which is equivalent to 50 miles. He practices twice a day, sometimes more if he's training at altitude. Phelps trains for around five to six hours a day, six days a week.

Michael Jordan said, "My attitude is if you push me towards something that you think is a weakness, then I will turn that perceived weakness into a strength" what can turn a weakness into strength self-discipline.

Both Michael Jordan and Michael Phelps their discipline for practice make them an icon of success in their respective professions. Michael Jordan won six NBA championship titles. Michael Phelps won twenty- eight Olympics medals: twenty-three gold, three silver, and two bronze. Self-discipline is the ability to deny oneself in pursuit of a goal. Self-Discipline is one of the essential skills that you need to succeed. It is also a challenging skill to develop but, when you do, the rewards are endless.

Scriptures tell us in Hebrews 12:11, "No discipline is fun while it lasts, but it seems painful at the time. Later, however, it yields the peaceful fruit of righteousness for those who have been trained by it."

Have you allowed yourself to be trained by discipline, or are you living precariously? Paul, the chief of the Apostles, said 1 Corinthians 9:24 & 27" Do you not know that in a race all the runners run, but only one gets the prize? Run in such a way as to get the prize. "No, I strike a blow to my body and make it my slave so that after I have preached to others, I will not be disqualified for the prize."

We should not be hasty to condemn successful people. Many of them went through the process and overcame that why they are where they are today. If you are willing to discipline yourself in your chosen pursuit, you will succeed. Success is not luck. It's discipline; successful people are not lucky they are disciplined. A poor man will save $300 to buy a Jordan sneaker so that he can impress his neighbor, while an entrepreneur save that same $300 to invest in something that will help his future.

We all know who will succeed between the two. It's not a matter of luck is a product of discipline. Both successful and unsuccessful are on the same earth breathe the same air but, one has the proper priority. It's said that most people who inherited wealth never make much of it many because of a lack of discipline. You need to discipline yourself if you must succeed. Most people

want to be Elon Musk, Bill Gates, or Jeff Bezos but, they forget that they did not get there by chance. They got there by making changes to their lives, sometimes inconveniencing themselves in pursuit of a brighter future. Bill Gates, in the early days of his business, he and his business partner use to spend countless hours and sleepless nights cording today their hard work and discipline paid off. Hate them or love them principles answer to anyone.

A young man said to Bishop Oyedepo, sir, I want to succeed like you. He said to the young man, "if you are workie like me, you will succeed like me." Another young man said to my spiritual father, Apostle Johnson Suleman. He said Apostle, I want to be as anointed as you are; he said to the young man, "if you are willing to do as I did, you will succeed." friend, it not by luck. It by discipline. Choose to be discipline today. You will get to the top in due time.

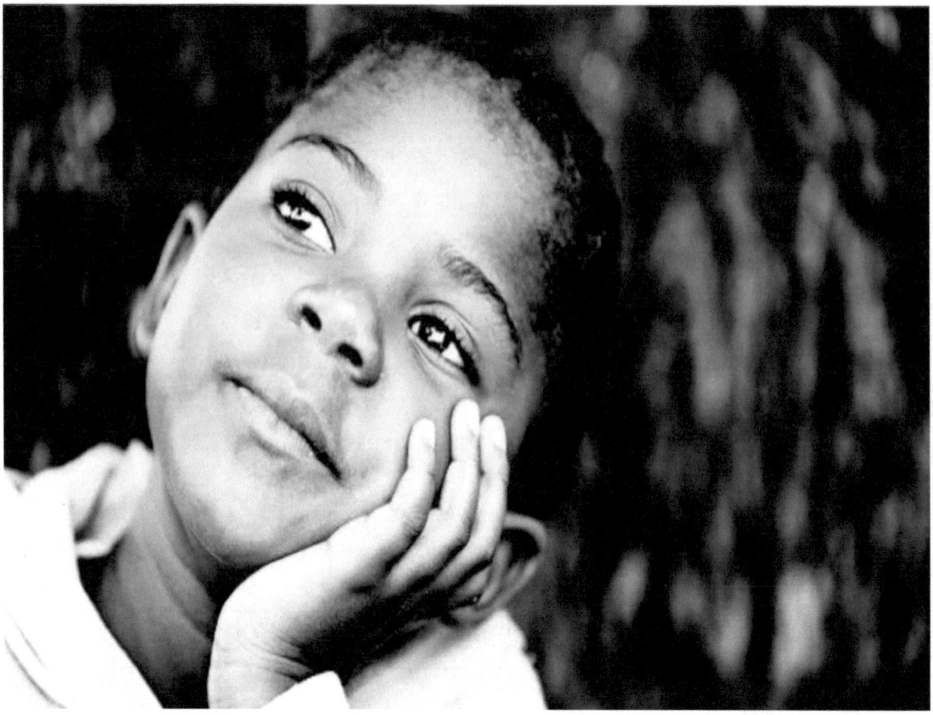

READING, STUDYING AND TIME DISCIPLINE

"Study to shew thyself approved." 2 Timothy 2:15a KJV

"As for these four young men, God gave them knowledge and skill in all literature and wisdom, and Daniel had understanding in all visions and dreams." Daniel 1:17 NKJV

"God gave these four young men an unusual aptitude for understanding every aspect of literature and wisdom.
And God gave Daniel the special ability to interpret the meanings of visions and dreams."Daniel 1:17 NLT

God gave them aptitude for learning just as he gave you aptitude for learning. There is no disadvantage in knowledge. Although discrimination and racism exist in some quarters in the past and still exist today, knowledge can be an equalizer. It can level the playing field. You have to acquire knowledge in all forms. Some of the richest in Forbes magazine are college drop-outs. But they did not throw away their appetite for knowledge. They still pursue learning outside of formal education. I am a big supporter of formal education. Everyone should acquire it if they can. Acquire all the degrees you can, but do not stop there; continue educating yourself. The day you stop learning, that is the day you start dying. Have you ever wondered why kids are always happy? I did until I discovered it is because they are always learning new things. No wonder Jesus said that if we must enter His kingdom, we must be humble and have the teachability of a child.

The richest man in finance, Warren Buffet, was once asked about the key to his success. He pointed to a stack of books and said, "I read 500 pages every day. That how knowledge work. He continues, it builds up, like compound interest. All of you can do it, but I guarantee not many of you will do it". Amongst other things, your future is determined by two things: The books you read and the people you interact with. Jeff Bezos, who is one of the richest men in the world, is an ardent reader. He carries a reading list of materials.

The wealthiest billionaire in the world, Bill Gates, reads one book per week. So he reads at least fifty books each year. Elon Musk, the CEO of Tesla and founder of the Boring Company, SolarCity, Skylink, Neuralink, and SpaceX, was asked how he learns to build rockets. He said, "I read books." Reading is so essential that Scriptures say: Daniel 9:2 ... "I Daniel understood by books the number of the years whereof the word of the Lord came to Jeremiah the prophet, that he would accomplish seventy years in the desolations of Jerusalem."

Scriptures say there that it was prophesied that Israel would come out of captivity after 70years. No one remembered it because it was hidden in books until Daniel found it. He used what he saw as a base for his prayers. What that says to me is that you could never discover certain things until you find them in books. Prayer is not effective without relevant knowledge. That means the gridlock you may be experiencing right now, the way out, maybe hidden in a book until you open and discover you may remain locked.

Bishop Oyedepo of winners said when God told him to start Covenant University, he had to research the university model he wanted and what he discovered is speaking today. Covenant University is one of the best in the world. He acquired information via reading discipline. My father in the faith, Prof. Johnson Suleman, is an addicted reader not only of God's word but other relevant materials.

Build your library according to your profession, career, or ministry. Read material that will help you in your chosen path.

Poor people read primarily for entertainment, while successful people read for self-improvement. I have heard many well, meaning believers say, "I only read the scriptures that is it." I highly recommend studying scriptures daily; at least three chapters for your daily enhancement. Besides, there are men and women that God has gifted in writing. Pick up their materials, assemble them, and you will be on your way. If you wait to invent the wheel, you may never drive the car.

Your success is in your reading and studying habits in addition to other things. You cannot rise or earn above your knowledge. We are often not paid for how we look. We get paid for how valuable our knowledge is. In Japanese philosophy, they call continuous improvement Kai-Zen or personal efficiency, etc. One of the ways you can improve yourself is through the discipline of reading or studying. It's not enough to read; it's also important to apply what we read or discovered through studying because we learn more by doing.

Time Discipline

"Redeeming the time because the days are evil."

Ephesians 5:16 KJV

We cannot get enough of it. Everyone needs it, and some wish they can control it, yet no one can stop it. It waits for no one. It is constant, and unstoppable. We must all learn to work with it. Everyone has the same amount of it. Wise use of "Time" is a challenge for many. It is impossible to recover when wasted. It is essential to make the most of its opportunities.

Now, allow me to summarize the history of time, according to secular scientists. The universe began with the Big Bang, about 15 billion years ago. The beginning of real-time would have been a singularity, at which the laws of physics would have broken down.

According to my Biblical world, view "time" began when God, the dual personality of both the father and mother of the time, spoke "time" into existence. The natural world, time & space as we know it came into being. In Genesis 1:1, in the beginning, God created the heavens and earth, Gen 1:3, and God said let there be light, and there was light. That's when "time" began. Gen 1:16 tells us how he regulates time. He made two lights the more excellent light to rule the day and the lesser light to rule the night etc. We live in a time-driven dispensation, we travel at the speed of sound, and we communicate at the speed of light. They say "time is money", but we can manage money, but we cannot manage time.

THINGS WE CAN'T DO WITH TIME:

We cannot manage "time". Time-Management is a fallacy (2) we can't control other people's time. We can only manage ourselves and the effective management of self-enhance productively and create more time for us.

> What we must focus on is not time management but self- management. There is nothing about "time management that makes more time for you this instant. When we set up calendars etc., we still have to do what is on them, and we will always use our time to do them.

2. What effective self-management does is this helps create time in the future. For example, if you do what you are supposed to do now. Assuming you are a teacher, You have school papers to grade today, and instead of putting them off for tomorrow You decide to do it right now by grading those papers today, You create more time for yourself tomorrow. You did not manage the time. You worked on yourself. It is still 24hrs tomorrow. In Prioritizing, we help increase productivity, and by increasing productivity, a product of self-management, we create more future time. Therefore, we have to work on ourselves to be more Time-disciplined. Come to think of it, there are things that we do in life that eat our time. Things that give us instant gratification or pleasure but no tangible benefits. For instance, excessive Facebook and Instagram usage, etc.

The problem with this generation is that there are so many distractions created to get her hooked or addicted. People spend a lot of time on social media instead of learning new skills or language. They waste time on unprofitable things. The time they should have used to improve their interpersonal relationships or pursue other gainful interests. You should limit your use and exposure to social media. Stop unnecessary smartphone usage.

Months back, I listened to an interview of a tech giant; the interviewer asked him if he uses his product as much as he should. He said: "the only time I had used it was when I tested it to make sure it works, and the day I did the presentation." Many millionaires and billionaires limit their children's electronics usage because they know how addictive smartphones & social media can be. When you discipline yourself by cutting down on your social media & likes. You create more time to work on things that benefit your tomorrow. Learn to say no to some invitations when you say yes to certain invitations. You create an infinite number of things you say No to that may have been of immense benefit to your overall goals in life. People may misinterpret you when you say 'NO! To them and that is ok. Your results will do the explaining.

"For the vision is yet for the appointed [future]

time it hurries toward the goal [of fulfillment]; it will not fail. Even though it delays, wait [patiently] for it, because it will certainly come; it will not delay."

HABAKKUK 2:3 AMP

Loyalty

Loyalty is measured in years.
A Proven track record to
a person or
organization shows
Loyalty and
commitment.

Loyalty

07

Loyalty is a commodity that is sought-after. Those that possess it are considered an asset. Some call those that have this quality old fashioned while fashion is about trends or what's famous sometimes particular popularity goes out of style. Still, this quality is relevant in any era. It's guaranteed to never go out of style. Sadly In many organizations and institutions today, it's almost absent. If your organization must succeed, you need people that have this quality. What am I talking about a seven-letter word Loyalty Scriptures admonished us in Proverbs 3:1-3 (NLT)

"My child, never forget the things I have taught

you. Store my commands in your heart. If you do this, you will

live for many years, and your life will be satisfying.

Never let loyalty and kindness leave you! Tie them around your neck as a reminder. Write them deep within your heart."

That's strong advice to everyone willing to listen "NEVER Let Loyalty and kindness leave you."

That's a strong one, 'Never' meaning, no time in your past, present, and future, not at all should you allow Loyalty to leave you. "Tie them around your neck as a reminder. Write them deep within your heart" in other words, earn a reputation for showing firm and constant support or allegiance to a person or institution. You should be known as a person who can be relied on when your name is measured; it should invoke a sense of confidence and pride in your character.

What is Loyalty?

It is defined as the quality of being loyal, loyal means to be faithful and devoted to someone or something. It comes from the French word fidéle, which means to be faithful, genuine, and trustworthy. Therefore, this is not Loyalty if someone is loyal to you because the law requires him/her. True loyalty comes from the heart. It's is not forced or coerced; you must earn loyalty. There are lots of people today that opportunity controls their commitment. Something is seriously wrong with your character if opportunity influences your Loyalty.

History of the word "loyalty" can be traced to the early 15th Century then it was defined as faithfulness to one's word or promise. "By the 16th century 1530's be precise the word evolved from a noun to an adjective loyal, at the same time the word had shifted, to towards "faithful allegiance to a sovereign or government." Thanks in part to feudalism. By the early 1600s, Loyalty and loyal both words became known as characterizing general devotion and dependability. Did you notice a pattern in the evolution of the word loyalty? It's taken almost three centuries for the word to evolve to what we recognize today fully.

Likewise, in character, a person cannot be loyal if he/she hasn't proven his faithfulness over time. Let me share with you a personal experience: Recently, I celebrated my birthday. For my birthday, we went out for evangelism with one of our members. We were ministering to people, doing evangelism, and sharing flyers. We shared material from one of our publications, namely, Rhema for living. We came across a certain lady, and I walked up to her, and I said, "madam, I want to invite you to church... here is our flyer." She said, "no, thank you." "I appreciate the gesture but, I belong to another church." "I have been there for 25years." Her confession warmed my heart, and I was immediately drawn to her because that is a quality I possess and admire in others. I said to her, "Mama remain loyal to your church and your Pastor. God bless you for standing by your man of God." That kind of devotion is rare in modern times. Loyalty is measured in years. A Proven track record to a person or organization shows Loyalty and commitment.

WHAT IS TRUE LOYALTY?

God is the true definition of Loyalty. Scriptures tell us in 2 Timothy 2:13, "If we are faithless, He remains faithful; He cannot deny Himself." True Loyalty is to remain faithful even when you have reasons to be faithless/disloyal. Scriptures also tell us in Matthew 28: 20B; and lo, I am with you always, even to the end of the age." Amen." A truly loyal person doesn't leave you when the going gets tough. They don't jump off your ship because it on fire. They are not a boat that can be tossed to and fro by every wind of challenge.

They stay together despite the challenges they face.

Something is wrong with someone's character if opportunity controls their loyalty.

True Loyalty is endless, and it does not have an expiration date. In our world today, many people just mouth loyalty, but it is not in their hearts. That is why we see today a man can get married and divorce tomorrow. There is no commitment to their wedding vows "to have and hold as long as they both shall live," and no allegiance. A Person stops being best buddies because their friend has nothing more to offer him. People stop going to church because their circumstances changed.
It's strange, but it's true that many people only show loyalty when it benefits them. A loyal man or a woman is priceless.

LOYALTY IN ORDER OF IMPORTANCE

1. Be loyal to God
2. Be loyal to your family (You husband or wife

and children are the first persons you must be loyal/devoted to after God.)

3. Be loyal to your church and your man of God.
4. Be loyal to your community.
5. Be loyal to your country.

THINGS YOU SHOULD KNOW ABOUT

Loyalty is not in words. It is in deeds. It is a lifestyle. Saying that you are loyal to a person or an organization does not quite cut it. It is measured in efforts, sweat, blood, and tears. Years of consistency, in season and out of season. Doing binding or putting together the best for the best interest of the object of your loyalty. It is proven that many businesses or organizations fail or die out within their first five years. Using that as a base. It's safe to say that the time frame we should begin to measure loyalty should be after five years.

(1) Loyalty is not only in the open, but it is also more so in secret: While a public confession of loyalty to a person or organization is ok. You should always be taken back by people that always sing your praises openly. Please! Please don't buy into that. Sometimes is a front for something else that's in some cases it not really what you are thinking. These verses of Scriptures come to mind,

John 2:23-25 "Now while he was in Jerusalem at the Passover Festival, many people saw the signs he was performing and believed in his name. But Jesus would not entrust himself to them, for he knew all people. He did not need any testimony about mankind, for he knew what was in each person." So, public loyalty is good, and personal loyalty /commitment is also significant (exemplary). The combination of both is greater than the sum of its parts. That's means it's even better when expresses together.

(2) Loyalty does not look for reward but deserves rewards: A truly loyal friend or employee hardly seeks rewards or recognition

though you know they deserve it. When someone starts telling you to see, "I'm loyal, give me this or that," that person, in most cases, does not deserve it, and if you cave-into his/her demand, and after she gets what she wants, she will undoubtedly leave you. Reward your loyal people! They don't need to ask for it. They deserve it.

(3)   Loyalty is a two-way street: If someone is loyal to you, you must also reciprocate by being faithful (Loyal) to

them. It is more effective when both parties are invested in it. Loyalty is more fruitful when faithfulness or commitment is flowing from both directions.

Can Loyalty be one way? The answer is Yes, and No?

Yes, It can be one-way, where one person or organization is putting all the effort doing all the heavy lifting it can work but, for a time. And No, it cannot be one-way because over time, when one party is not reciprocating (receiving what they gave) loyalty will become strained, and if the trend continues down that part, it may eventually faze out.

In other words, the person that was loyal to you will stop being Loyal (faithful). Let us face it when we give something, we expect something back in return, and if we do not get benefits from our investment in anything, we tend to drawback. That's just how life works.

Extreme of Loyalty: Blind loyalty

The extreme of anything is dangerous. There must be a healthy balance in other for you to maintain your sanity. The word blind connotes disability, and there is no such thing as blind Loyalty. If it's blind, it's not loyalty. To be loyal (loyalty) is a conscious decision one makes to follow a Person or organization.

WHAT YOU MUST DO TO EARN LOYALTY

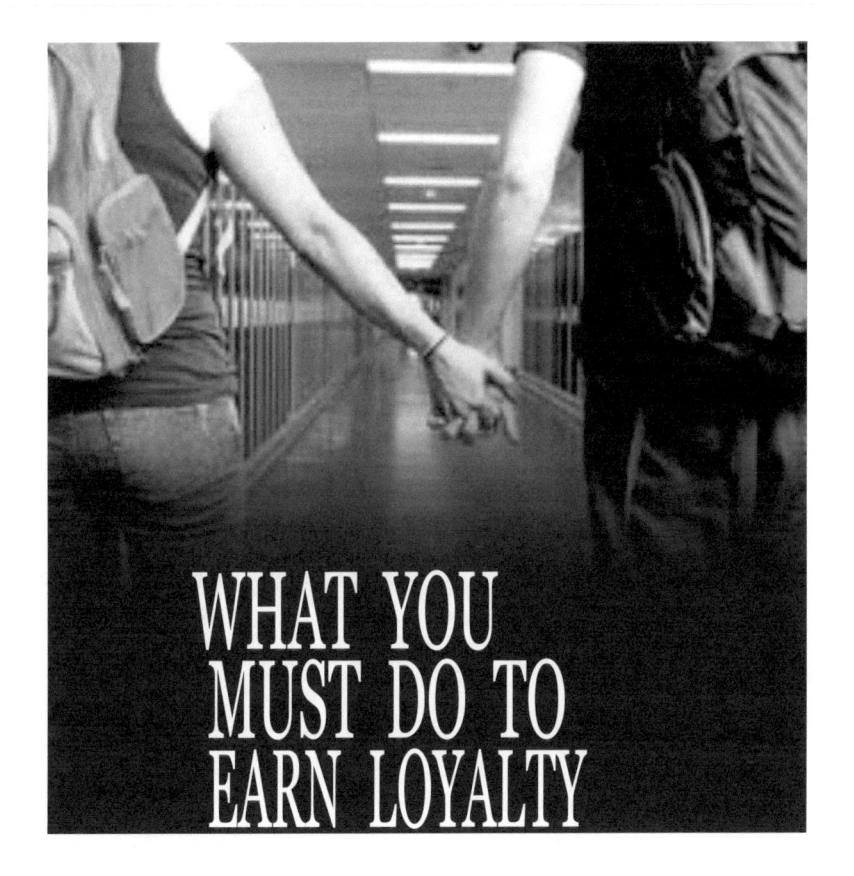

CULTIVATE IT IN PEOPLE (Develop it in people)

These are suggestions I believe can be helpful to you, but a word of caution first. It is by no means an appeasement. These are common-sense strategy that works & must not be used to manipulate others.

Wisdom is profitable to direct. It's a fact that anyone can learn to be loyal if they choose to, but we can do things to make it easy for others to be loyal.

1. Be yourself, be sincere and genuine. Most people love a man or woman that has integrity lets you yes be yes, and your no is no.

2. Be decisive and consistent. Be uncompromising and flexible when necessary.

3. Help people and do not ever ask them to pay you back.

4. If you are in a place of power, don't abuse it; use it as a platform for good.

5. Be genuinely interested in people, don't be weird.

6. Do not take them for granted. I mean that if you benefit from someone's help, efforts, or presence without showing that you are grateful and appreciative, that's taking them for granted.

7. Respect their opinion and ask for their input (if you are in a team setting) Admire and celebrate them.

Celebrate or appreciate your friends or workers from the heart sometimes through gifts, not manipulation but in appreciation. If you in a place of power, organize an outing, appreciation weekend. Reward them for a job well done etc.

If we don't take a stand for what is right, we will soon find ourselves in a dystopian society

8

▶ Break THE LIMIT

Morality | 08
break the limits

"Therefore, whatever you want men to do to you, do also to them, for this is the Law and the Prophets."
    Matthew 7:12 NKJV

"Do not be deceived: "Evil Company corrupts good habits." 1 Corinthians 15:33 NKJV

We live in an era where the rules of life have been

constantly rewritten, in an age where the wrong or bad ideas are a daily challenge to fundamental principles. If we don't take a stand for what is right, we may soon find ourselves in a dystopian society. In a culture where some say "out with the old, and in with the new." But old does not always mean outdated. Certain principles transcend times.

Scriptures say, Thus said the LORD: "Stand in the ways and see, and ask for the old paths, where the good way is, and walk in it; Then you will find rest for your souls. But they said, we will not walk in it." Jeremiah 6:16. One of that old path" and a good way is what we are going to discuss in this chapter. We are going to be shedding some light on Morality through a biblical lens. We may differ in how we approach this subject because it's a controversial subject, but we can all agree that Morality is vital in our society.

WHAT IS MORALITY?

Morality (n)/Moral (adj) it's a principle, a system of values that helps us distinguish between right and wrong.

Now, let's talk about terminologies for a second. Generally, Morality and ethics are used interchangeably in philosophy, meaning the same: right or wrong.

WHAT IS ETHICS?

Ethics is a right and wrong standard imposed by a society based on what cultures or societies say. So ethics are acceptable behaviors or norms. For Instance, it's unethical to lie on your job application or cheat on your spouse's (husband or wife).

There are two kinds of ethics; Descriptive ethics & prescriptive ethics. We may talk about them in volume two. While Ethics is external, Morality is internal.

MORALITY: Standards of right and wrong base on our value system. A moral compass is our inbuilt value system. To some degree, our ethics inform our morals; also, the nurture and nature we discussed in an earlier chapter can inform our morals. For example, it's immoral to take what belongs to another forcefully. Furthermore, we can argue that certain morals are inborn, like love, compassion, etc. A step further, we can say that's Morality results from our subscription to specific values.

You may say, Pastor, I don't need God to be a good person. Friend, you are right. You can be good without believing in God but, YOU CAN'T BE GOOD ACCORDING TO DIVINE STANDARDS WITHOUT GOD. Philosophers of antiquity: Aristotle, Augustine, Aquinas, Imhotep. George Washington recognized that our morals come from a higher power. It was noted that George Washington said: "It is impossible to rightly govern a nation without God and the Bible."

WHAT OR WHO GAVE US OUR MORAL AUTHORITY?

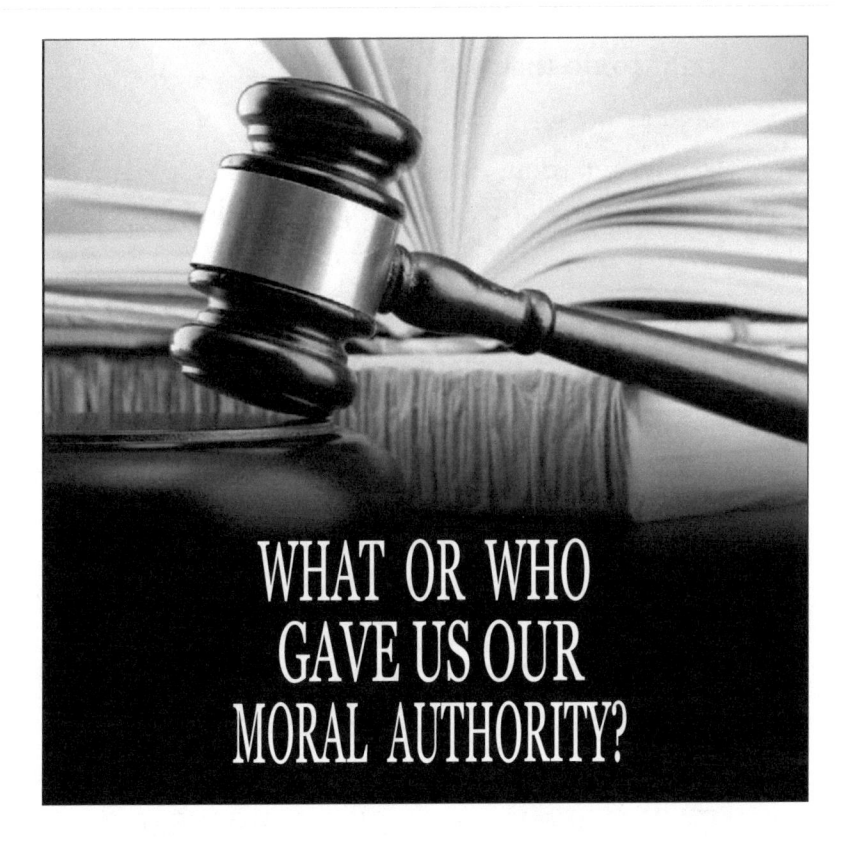

Everything created has a source. For example, police have the authority to arrest a criminal. Where did the police get that right? Police derive their power from the state or local government. Where did the local government or state get their authority? The provincial government or state gets its authority from the federal government. Where did the federal government derive its jurisdiction (Power)? The federal government derives its authority from the Constitution. How did the Constitution come to be? The people empower the

Constitution. Where did the people get the right to do that?

People get their rights from God. My point? We need a source for everything, including Morality.

THE QUESTION MUST BE, ASK THEM WHY GOD? GOD IS THE OBJECTIVE REFERENCE POINT.

WHY AN OBJECTIVE REFERENCE POINT?
WITHOUT AN OBJECTIVE REFERENCE POINT, THERE IS NO WAY OF KNOWING WHAT IS GOOD OR BAD, RIGHT OR WRONG, UP OR DOWN.

WHY GOD? Because of HIS NATURE, GOD IS GOOD.
Therefore, He is THE STANDARD by which we must measure our value.

HE IS THE ULTIMATE MORAL AUTHORITY. For
example, without the Ten Commandments, we will not know that to kill is evil, Morality will be whatever we think is right, and sometimes what is suitable for me may not be right for you.

If there is no objective reference point, Morality will only be subjective. Subject to personal opinions. An instance occurred in scriptures.

Genesis 4:8-9 Now, Cain said to his brother Abel, "Let's go out to the field." While they were in the field, Cain attacked his brother Abel and killed him. Then the Lord said to Cain, "Where is your brother Abel?" "I don't know," he replied. "Am I my brother's keeper?"

Kane wore three hats in this Scripture. He was the Judge, jury, and executioner. He acted as the moral authority and handed judgment based on what he perceived to be correct.

Without a moral reference point, we do what we think is right in doing so; Morality becomes subjective. It becomes subject to our interpretation but, certain morals need no private interpretation example: "Thou shall not kill," there is no further need for personal interpretation. It the same today, tomorrow, and all time. It applies to everyone regardless of gender, ethnicity, nationality, religious affiliation, etc. It is self-explanatory. Let us ask another question.

WHY DO YOU NEED MORALS?

Please take a look at history. You will notice that every civilization lives by a set of codes or moral standards. However, primitive, it is well documented that any society that forsakes its moral ends up ruins. For example, the Egyptian empire, the Persian Empire, and the Roman Empire, etc.

These civilizations collapsed, amongst other things,

because of the eroding of certain morals. Lack of Morality or ethics eats up the fabric of any society. When people begin to call good evil and evil good, that's a severe problem. These civilizations use to care for the "least of these," but they got to the point where power becomes more important than their citizens' well being. Whenever a society puts profit over people, that society is heading for a collision course. May God help us all in Jesus's name.

BENEFITS OF MORALITY.

Morality creates and helps us maintain a stable and peaceful society, etc. Therefore, the lack of it, minus the source, leads to self-implosion and degradation.

CAN HUMAN BE THE SOURCE FOR MORALITY? The short answer is no. THE LAST TIME WE ALLOW HUMAN TO BE THE SOURCE FOR MORALITY OR MORAL AUTHORITY, we produce dictators like Adolf Hitler and Joseph Stalin. Hitler and Stalin claimed tens of millions of lives. In World War I, 17million people were killed, and World War two claimed 73million lives. Stalin killed 20 million Russians, and Hitler killed over 5 million Jews, and between both of them, 110 million lives were lost.

As imperfect beings, we cannot be the moral authority. The question, WHAT ARE YOUR MORALS AND WHO IS YOUR MORAL AUTHORITY?

"according to the Biblical account, there are only two genders: male and female.

09

Break THE LIMIT

God's view on Gender & Sexuality | 09

Genesis 1:27, Amplified Bible, Classic Edition

"So God created man in His own image; in the image and likeness of God, He created him; male and female, He created them."

Hebrews 4:12 Amplifed Bible, Classic Edition

"For the Word that God speaks is alive and full of power

[making it active, operative, energizing, and effective]; it is sharper than any two-edged sword, penetrating to the dividing line of the breath of life (soul) and [the immortal] spirit, and of joints and marrow [of the deepest parts of our nature], exposing and sifting and

analyzing and judging the very thoughts and purposes of the heart."

It's wonderful to know that God and his word do not change, even when society tends to teeter on the brink of collapse.

Even when social norms tend to change in every generation, there is one source of truth we can rely on to point us in the right direction. It's called the word of God, the living and breathing scriptures.

As of this writing, there are 81 genders and counting. However, according to the Biblical account, there are only two genders: male and female. Genesis 1:27. There are no three, four, five, hundred, etc.; there are only two. The above, scripture is grounded in biology and reality. Two plus two equals four in every language. It doesn't matter what the latest trend is or what the present regime seeks to legislate.

You cannot legislate the truth,

> *1 Corinthians 13:8, KJV "for we can do nothing against the truth but for the truth."*

> **John 8:35: "The Scripture cannot be set aside, cancelled, broken, *or* annulled" (AMPC).**

The fact is this: if a person, male or female, lived for one hundred years and died, and three hundred years later, if they dig up his or her bones, they can only identify two genders: male or female. It doesn't matter what they called themselves when they walked the Earth.

Please hear me; my goal is not to delegitimize how someone feels. If someone believes what they are feeling is real, then, intellectually, I cannot argue how they felt; feelings are personal. On the other hand, I believe facts and reality should take precedence over feelings.

This is the fact, or reality. The Bible primarily acknowledges and presents two genders: male and female. In the creation account we found in Genesis, it states that God created humankind in His image, male and female (Genesis 1:27).

This passage states a binary, or only two possible understandings of gender; it recognizes the distinctiveness and complementarity of male and female.

Throughout the scriptures, gender roles and expectations are often discussed within the context of marriage, family, and community. There are passages that address the responsibilities and roles of husbands and wives, parents and children, and leaders within the faith community. For example

Ephesians 5:25-33

"Husbands, love your wives, as Christ loved the church and

gave Himself up for her. So that He might sanctify her, having cleansed her by the washing of water with the Word, That He might present the church to Himself in glorious splendor, without spot, wrinkle, or any such thing [that she might be holy and faultless]. Even so, husbands should love their wives as if they were, in a sense, their own bodies. He who loves his own wife loves himself. For no man ever hated his own flesh, but nourishes, carefully protects, and cherishes it, as Christ does the church, Because we are members (parts) of His body. For this reason, a man shall leave his father and his mother and be joined to his wife, and the two shall become one flesh. This mystery is very great, but I speak concerning the relationship between Christ and the church. However, let each man of you [without exception] love his wife as [in a sense] his very own self; and let the wife see that she respects and reverences her husband, that she notices him, regards him, honors him, prefers him, venerates him, and esteems him, and that she defers to him, praises him, and loves and admires him exceedingly.

The above passages of scripture are self-explanatory. It outlines some of the Roles and responsibilities of both sexes. It compares Christ and the church with husband and wife. Christ's or the husband's duty is to love the wife as Christ loved the church and nourish and protect her, and wives are to honor their husbands. "Let the wife see that she respects *and* reverences her husband; that she notices him, regards him, honors him, prefers him, venerates him, and esteems him; and that she defers to him, praises him, and loves and admires him exceedingly."

Parents and Children: Ephesians 6:1-3

"Children, obey your parents in the Lord, for this is right. Honor thy father and mother, which is the first commandment with a promise; That it may be well with you, and thou mayest live long on the earth."

Leaders and faith community: Hebrews 13:17–19

"Obey them that have the rule over you, and submit yourselves; for they watch for your souls, as they must give account, that they may do it with joy and not with grief, for that is unprofitable for you. Pray for us, for we trust we have a good conscience and are willing to live honestly in all things. But I beseech you rather to do this, that I may be restored to you sooner."

More scriptures that address gender roles within marriage, family, and the community:

Genesis 2:20-24 *"So Adam gave names to all cattle, to the birds of the air, and to every beast of the field. But for Adam, there was no helper comparable to him. And the LORD God caused a deep sleep to fall on Adam, and he slept; and He took one of his ribs and closed up the flesh in its place. Then the rib that the LORD God had taken from man, He made into a woman, and He brought her to the man. And Adam said, "This is now bone of my bones and flesh of my flesh; she shall be called Woman, because she was taken out of Man." Therefore a man shall leave his father and mother and be joined to his wife, and they shall become one flesh."*

Titus 2:4–8 says *"that they admonish the young women to love their husbands, to love their children, to be discreet, chaste, homemakers, good, and obedient to their own husbands, that the word of God may not be blasphemed. Likewise, exhort the young men to be sober-minded, in all things showing yourself to be a pattern of good works; in doctrine showing integrity, reverence, incorruptibility, and sound speech that cannot be condemned, that one who is an opponent may be ashamed, having nothing evil to say of you."*

Timothy 3:2 *"A bishop then must be blameless, the husband of one wife, temperate, sober-minded, of good behavior, hospitable, and able to teach."*

Ephesians 4:28, King James Version (KJV)

"Let him that stole steal no more; but rather let him labor, working with his hands the thing that is good, that he may have to give to him that needeth."

It's very important to note that the Bible does not provide an exploration of gender identities beyond male and female as understood in its cultural and historical context. Every time gender or sexuality is measured in the scriptures, it refers to the relationship between one man and one woman in the context of a marital relationship. In Scripture, any sexual relationship that is talked about outside of marriage is referred to as sin. For example:

Jude 7 *"[The wicked are sentenced to suffer] just as Sodom and Gomorrah and the adjacent towns—which likewise gave themselves over to impurity and indulged in unnatural vice and sensual perversity—are laid out [in plain sight] as an exhibit of perpetual punishment [to warn] of everlasting fire."*

Allow me to restate the previous statement in a different way: anytime a sexual relationship that is not between one man and one woman in the context of a marriage relationship is measured in the scriptures, it's referred to as a sinful relationship. Whether it is heterosexual, homosexual, lesbian, etc. It's sin, period. Though the main purpose of this chapter is not to discuss sexual preferences, that's another topic entirely. The scriptures are clear about sexual explorations or preferences. Here are a few scriptures on that topic:

Hebrews 13:4: *"Let marriage be held in honor (esteemed worthy, precious, of great price, and especially dear) in all things. And thus let the marriage bed be undefiled (kept un-dishonored); for God will judge and punish the unchaste [all guilty of sexual vice] and adulterous."*

Undefiled is another word for sexual purity. Sex outside of marriage is forbidden. Also, is sexual vice or sexual exploration clear enough?

Another scripture:

Romans 1:24-27 *"Therefore God gave them up in the lusts of their [own] hearts to sexual impurity, to the dishonoring of their bodies among themselves [abandoning them to the degrading power of sin], Because they exchanged the truth of God for a lie and worshiped and served the creature rather than the Creator, Who is blessed forever! Amen (so be it). For this reason, God gave them over and abandoned them to vile affections and degrading passions. For their women, who exchanged their natural function for an unnatural and abnormal one, And the men also turned from natural relations with women and were set ablaze (burning out, consumed) with lust for one another—men committing shameful acts with men and suffering in their own bodies and personalities the inevitable consequences and penalty of their wrongdoing and going astray, which was their fitting retribution."*

Like we stated earlier, every form of sexual relationship outside of God's design, which is marriage, is equally sinful. Moreover, we must understand that humanity outside of Christ will always wrestle with the consequences of the fall. The solution begins and ends with faith in God's free gift of salvation from all forms of vice.

MODERN UNDERSTANDING OF GENDER/SEX

Now, contemporary understandings of gender as a spectrum or the existence of diverse gender identities are a modern phenomenon. The term gender identity was coined by psychiatry professor Robert J. Stoller in 1964 and popularized by psychologist John Money. Who was John Money? John Money was a New Zealand-born American psychologist, sexologist, and professor at Johns Hopkins University known for his controversial research on human sexual behavior and gender. Money established the Johns Hopkins Gender Identity Clinic, the first clinic in the United States to perform sexual reassignment surgeries. Money believes that gender is learned rather than innate.

When we engage with the topic of gender, we must approach it through the lens of scripture. We must be careful not to bend scripture to fit an agenda. I personally adhere to a traditional understanding of gender based on biblical texts, while others adopt more worldly views that affirm and support individuals with diverse gender identities. While the latter may sound good. However, to identify as a gender/Sex other than that which is scriptural is contradictory to God's word. The beauty of the word is this: it has the ability to transform an Individual from the inside out.

2 Corinthians 3:18 *"And all of us, as with unveiled faces, [because we] continued to behold [in the Word of God] as in a mirror the glory of the Lord, are constantly being transfigured into His very own image in ever increasing splendor and from one degree of glory to another; for this comes from the Lord [Who is] the Spirit."*

MY OBSERVATION

This is an observation: every time I hear this topic on gender affirmation, the subject of personal encounters with the Lord is completely left out. I personally believe that, as a minister, it is our duty to help individuals encounter Jesus. One genuine encounter with Jesus will erase a lifetime of struggle. The Christianity of today, especially in the West, is full of showmanship instead of a genuine encounter that will bring men and women back into fellowship with the Holy Spirit. Some ministers today gather people unto themselves and not unto Christ Jesus. This is a fact: the church of old had the same challenges we face today, but they were able to handle them because they knew where their loyalties lay.

Another thing I have noticed is the prayerlessness of the church. Today, church is full of extracurricular activities, and prayer has taken a backseat. The church of old understood the need for consecration; they understood the need for circumcision of the flesh. The church of today is mainly focused on the M.B. and C. of ministries. Member, building, and cash There are few churches today that have made prayer and fasting a lifestyle. Some have made activities their only focus. Therefore, the Spirit of God has moved out and the flesh has moved in. The state of society tells you the condition of the church. My father in the Lord Apostle. Prof. Johnson Suleman said, "The Church of old was in the upper room agonizing, while the church of today is in the supper room organizing."

WHAT ARE THE ROLES OF THE BELIEVER IN ADDRESSING THIS ISSUES?

When it comes to teaching on gender, believers have the awesome responsibility to approach this topic with sensitivity and from a sound biblical perspective. What scripture teaches must not be downplayed in order to fit certain contexts or narratives. Hear some suggestions or guidelines.

1. BIBLICAL DOGMA

Our dogmas must be based on sound Biblical principles. We must not be emotional or act under pressure. Let the word and the Spirit guide you. That's why God gave us the Holy Spirit and His word to guide us. Therefore, we must base our argument on foundational truths such as the creation account in Genesis.

Genesis 1:26-27, which affirms the nature of male and female There are relevant biblical passages that address gender roles within marriage, family, and the faith community. Such

Genesis 2:20-24 *"So Adam gave names to all cattle, to the birds of the air, and to every beast of the field. But for Adam, there was no helper comparable to him. And the LORD God caused a deep sleep to fall on Adam, and he slept; and He took one of his ribs and closed up the flesh in its place. Then the rib that the LORD God had taken from man, He made into a woman, and He brought her to the man. And Adam said, "This is now bone of my bones and flesh of my flesh; she shall be called Woman, because she was taken out of Man." Therefore a man shall leave his father and mother and be joined to his wife, and they shall become one flesh."*

Titus 2:4–8 says *"that they admonish the young women to love their husbands, to love their children, to be discreet, chaste, homemakers, good, and obedient to their own husbands, that the word of God may not be blasphemed. Likewise, exhort the young men to be sober-minded, in all things showing yourself to be a pattern of good works; in doctrine showing integrity, reverence, incorruptibility, and sound speech that cannot be condemned, that one who is an opponent may be ashamed, having nothing evil to say of you."*

1 Timothy 3:2 *"A bishop then must be blameless, the husband of one wife, temperate, sober-minded, of good behavior, hospitable, and able to teach."*

Ephesians 4:28, King James Version (KJV) *"Let him that stole steal no more; but rather let him labor, working with his hands the thing that is good, that he may have to give to him that needeth."*

2. GENDER IS BY DESIGN

Genesis 1:26-27 Amplified Bible, Classic Edition

"God said, Let Us [Father, Son, and Holy Spirit] make mankind in Our image, after Our likeness, and let them have complete authority over the fish of the sea, the birds of the air, the [tame] beasts, and over all of the earth, and over everything that creeps upon the earth. So God

created man in His own image; in the image and likeness of God, He created him; male and female, He created them."

According to the above scriptures, male and female gender is by design. We are God's design and therefore carries dignity within. I believe no man or woman is beyond redemption. We must emphasize that all individuals, regardless of gender, are created in the image of God and possess inherent dignity, worth, and value. Teach about the mutual respect and partnership that should exist between men and women in the context of relationships, family, and society.

3. WE MUST EXERCISE CHRIST'S LOVE.

John 13:34-35, Amplified Bible, Classic Edition

"I give you a new commandment: that you should love one another. Just as I have loved you, you too should love one another. By this shall all [men] know that you are my disciples, if you love one another [if you keep on showing love among yourselves]?"

We are called Christians. One who has taken on the identity of Christ We must therefore exercise Christ-like love. We must teach the importance of imitating Christ's love, compassion, and acceptance towards all people, not necessarily their sinful lifestyle but their individuality. Emphasize the need for communities that embrace individuals with diverse views and treat them with respect and dignity.

1. CULTURAL DISCERNMENT

Romans 12:1-2 *"I appeal to you therefore, brethren, and beg of you, in view of [all] the mercies of God, to make a decisive dedication of your bodies [presenting all your members and faculties] as a living sacrifice, holy (devoted, consecrated), and well-pleasing to God, which is your reasonable (rational, intelligent) service and spiritual worship. Do not be conformed to this world (this age), [fashioned after and adapted to its external, superficial customs], but be transformed (changed) by the [entire] renewal of your mind [by its new ideals and its new attitude], so that you may prove [for yourselves] what is the good and acceptable and perfect will of God, even the thing that is good and acceptable and perfect [in His sight for you]."*

We must help congregants navigate cultural influences and societal debates around gender. Encourage critical thinking based on reality and discernment while remaining grounded in biblical principles. We are called to transformation, not conformity. Society isn't supposed to influence us; it's the other way around. We must not seek to be politically correct; we must seek to be scripturally compliant. Jesus was counterculture, and so should we be. (Counterculture: a way of life and attitudes opposed to or at variance with the prevailing social norm.)

2. PASTORAL CARE AND SUPPORT

Jeremiah 3:15 *"And I will give you pastors according to my heart, who shall feed you with knowledge and understanding."*

John 21:17 *"He saith unto him the third time, Simon, son of Jonas, lovest thou me? Peter was grieved because he said to him the third time, Lovest thou me? And he said unto him, Lord, thou knowst all things; thou knowst that I love thee. Jesus saith unto him, Feed my sheep."*

Pastors are called to feed their flocks. We must recognize that individuals within the congregation may have personal struggles or questions related to gender identity. We must offer pastoral care and support that is grounded in compassion and a safe space for discussions, counseling, and prayers. Connect individuals to resources or support networks as needed.

3. UNITY AND DIALOGUE

John 17:21-23 *"That they all may be one, [just] as You, Father, are in Me and I in You, that they also may be one in Us, so that the world may believe and be convinced that You have sent Me. I have given to them the glory and honor which you have given me that they may be one [even] as we are one: I in them and You in Me, in order that they may become one and perfectly united, that the world may know and [definitely] recognize that You sent Me and that You have loved them [even] as You have loved Me."*

Unity and dialogue: Foster an environment where respectful dialogue and understanding can take place, even when there are differing viewpoints on gender-related topics. Encourage open conversations that seek to build bridges and promote unity within the body of Christ. The goal is to point people to the scriptures and allow the scriptures to be the final authority.

In conclusion, it is important for Ministers and pastors to prayerfully study and seek wisdom in their teaching, recognizing the complexity and sensitivity of the topic of gender. Each believer must approach it according to the leading of the inner witness, and we must avoid reading meaning into the scriptures and allow the text to interpret itself. God knew that we would get to this moment in time and has made provision in the Word for such a time. As we strive to embody Christ's love and grace in our interactions with others.

salvation
PRAYER

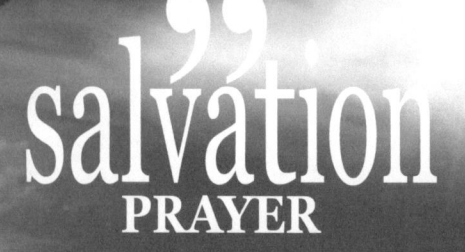

If this book has touched your life and you want to give your life to Christ, please pray this prayer with me:

Father in Heaven, I am a sinner in need of your salvation. I believe that your son Jesus Christ died on the cross for my trespasses and sin. I believe he was buried, and the third day he rose from the dead for my salvation, and he lives for my justification. Dearest

Jesus, come into my heart. Be my Lord and personal savior. Lord Holy Spirit, help me to live for God. Thank you, Father, thank you Jesus, and thank you Holy Spirit I am born again, Amen. Welcome TO THE FAMILY OF GOD.

Now that you have prayed that prayer. Know this; you cannot live the God-life on your strength. It takes the empowerment of the Holy Spirit to guide and help you.

Read your Bible daily. Start with the New Testament and look for Bible-believing and praying church and attend services. So you grow in God.

PRAYER OF rededication

My dearest Father, I humble myself before you today. I confess my sin. I want to thank you for hearing my prayers and helping me return to you. I had put confidence in everyone, including myself. As you know, it has not been working out. I see where I have been going the wrong way-my own way. *Dear Lord, I return to you as the Bible says, Zachariah 1:3, "return to me and I will return to you". 1 John 1:9 if I confess my sin, you are faithful and just to forgive me. I pray for your guidance as I listen to your voice. Let me return to what is important to you. Help my attitudes to change. Instead of focusing on myself and circumstances to meet my needs, I can turn to you and find love, purpose, and divine direction. Matthew 6:33" seek you first the kingdom and righteousness" help me seek you first and your purpose. Let my relationship with you be the most important thing in my life. Thank you, father, thank you Jesus, and thank you precious Holy Spirit, Amen.*

Made in the USA
Columbia, SC
21 October 2024